reply requested

30 letters of advice
Richard Yorkey

▲ **ADDISON-WESLEY PUBLISHING COMPANY**

Reading, Massachusetts • Menlo Park, California
Don Mills, Ontario • Wokingham, England • Amsterdam
Sydney • Singapore • Tokyo • Madrid • Bogota
Santiago • San Juan

CREDITS: p. 21, Wide World Photos; p. 29, Reprinted by permission of the Chicago Tribune—New York News Syndicate, Inc.; p. 32, Joseph C. Oakes; p. 46, MOMMA by Mell Lazarus, Courtesy of Mell Lazarus and Field Newspaper Syndicate; p. 49, William L. Smith

ISBN 0-201-10078-9
11 12 13 14 15-AL-96 95 94 93

Contents

TO THE TEACHER

The purpose of these letters is to motivate real communication practice. Students read authentic letters to Ann Landers and meet the challenge to write their own replies. They also practice speaking skills by discussing each problem and by role-playing.

Whatever special purpose and procedures you adopt for your class, some of the ideas suggested here may be interesting and useful. Activities for each letter and reply include: Vocabulary, Factual Questions, Cultural Notes, Language Use, Discussion, Language in Life, and Writing. There are various ways in which the reading and writing activities can be handled; the particular approach depends on the class and the time available.

READING

The letters are short enough to be read in class. Since no letter is longer than 250 words, two or three minutes should be sufficient for silent reading. There may be times when you prefer to assign a letter to be read and a reply written outside of class. In either case, students should be encouraged to use a dictionary and be sure that they understand the meaning of unfamiliar words and expressions.

VOCABULARY

The vocabulary that has been isolated for each letter includes words and expressions that are likely to be unfamiliar or that are central to comprehension of the problem. Depending on your class and your particular teaching strategy, you can introduce these before or discuss them after the letter is read. Challenging students to guess meanings from context is useful at the high intermediate and advanced levels.

Personally, I like to have students bring a dictionary to class. This should be an up-to-date English-English dictionary, preferably one prepared specifically for ESL students. The language of these letters is direct and informal. Many of the words are labeled in dictionaries as *slang, colloquial, informal,* or even *nonstandard.* It is useful for ESL students to discover that a dictionary is not a sacred book in which only the best, most literary words are recorded. A great deal of listening and speaking practice can be achieved through the discussion of word meanings and usage and the frequent differences among dictionaries.

FACTUAL QUESTIONS

This section makes sure that students have understood the factual details of the situation. Inferences and value judgments come later in the DISCUSSION section. The answers to these questions may overlap; the important thing is to be sure that all of the facts have been understood.

You might challenge students to report the situation by giving an oral or written summary. A factual summary is a productive exercise because it requires accurate reading comprehension, appropriate choice of words, and carefully controlled syntax. However, students must be carefully prepared to handle reported speech before they undertake a summary of this kind. To clarify who's who and avoid awkward references or circumlocutions, students should agree on personal names for the characters. It might also be interesting to compare some of the summaries to reveal different ways of expressing the same ideas. Stylistic variations can also be analyzed for accuracy and appropriateness.

CULTURAL NOTES

Whenever they seem appropriate or necessary, informative comments are included that direct attention to American practices or attitudes that may differ in other countries. The teacher is the best judge of whether this information should be developed in detail.

LANGUAGE USE

Occasionally, an interesting or unusual instance of diction is pointed out. This may be an example of slang, an idiom, or the distinction between words like *come* and *go*. In some cases, levels of language (or "registers") are explained and practiced, such as degrees of politeness or different ways to express doubt or disbelief.

DISCUSSION

Discussion questions direct students' attention to the larger, socio-cultural issues involved. This is a chance for students to make inferences and to express their own values. Most often this discussion should precede the writing of replies; but sometimes you may want students to write their replies without too much discussion or too many ideas from other students. With some letters, there may be unanimous agreement, but with many there is likely to be divided opinion and strongly expressed viewpoints.

While much of the success of class discussions depends on spontaneity and enthusiasm, some preparation is advisable in order to avoid aimless conversation or endless argument. There need not be the formal structure of a debate (although this procedure may be an interesting change of pace), but the discussion should be controlled enough to allow for maximum participation and courteous respect for differing ideas.

LANGUAGE IN LIFE

This section introduces students to some of the common functions of language. Students express the language functions in paired practice or by role-playing. Many of the exercises are based on reference materials prepared for the Council of Europe and published by J.A. van Ek in *The Threshold Level for Modern Language Learning in Schools* (London: Longman, 1977). Some of the language functions included in these letters are persuading, giving and refusing permission, and expressing anger, blame, preference, surprise, displeasure, embarrassment, sympathy, and sarcasm.

LANGUAGE IN LIFE activities are divided into sections. Sections marked with a single star (★) are intended for all students. Sections marked with double stars (★★) are intended for high intermediate and advanced students. Of course, some double star activities may be profitably used by lower intermediate students.

WRITING

The traditional way of handling writing assignments is to collect and correct them, without sharing them with the students in class. There are two disadvantages, particularly for the kind of writing that is practiced in these letters. First, students are "doing a writing assignment for the teacher" rather than genuinely communicating their ideas to a real audience which is, because of the shared reading experience, involved and possibly committed to a different idea. Second, students benefit from only the teacher's comments and corrections when this method is employed. It's important to remember that the response of the students' peers is socially important, and their corrections are possibly pedagogically more reinforcing than any the teacher could make.

Letters can be distributed at random in class so that each student has a letter written by some other student. Each student is then asked to read the letter silently and write a response to the *content*. This may be agreement or disagreement with the view expressed by the writer and the reason for the reader's judgment. Each student may also be asked to react to the *form* of the letter—the vocabulary, grammar, and general effectiveness. At the beginning this may simply be "fault-finding." As students become more experienced with this procedure, they tend to move from finding only proofreading errors to expressing genuine criticism of content and style.

Since writing and criticizing are responsible acts of communication, student editors should be asked to identify themselves. Each letter may then be returned to its writer, who should have time to read the comments before the letters are turned in to the teacher.

Impress upon students that the letters will be circulated in class. Everyone will see the quality of handwriting and the standard of English, so they should write as carefully and correctly as possible.

Ann Landers' replies are short, sometimes no more than 25 words. Occasionally a very short reply may be stylistically effective. For practice, however, students should write more than this; a single, well-constructed paragraph is best. But again, I would stress the importance of quality rather than quantity—without frustrating the students' natural enthusiasm.

ANN LANDERS' REPLY

Once the students' letters have been read and commented on, they should read the reply which Ann Landers actually wrote. Her reply often leads to further interaction in class because of disagreement or differing interpretations and values.

MOTIVATION

Students are often motivated to write letters in which they ask for advice about some personal problem of their own—for example, a noisy roommate, a nosey in-law, Americans who ask embarrassing or ignorant questions, or the dull, tasteless food in the cafeteria. Each letter can be given to another student in class who, like Ann Landers, offers advice in a written reply. For speaking rather than writing practice, students enjoy playing the role of a radio adviser who gives advice orally to students who "telephone in."

Few international students who have used this material were familiar with Ann Landers' column. However, almost all of them were familiar with advice-to-the-lovelorn and similar advice columns in their national newspapers. Letters like these, it seems, are a kind of folk literature in many languages. If the Ann Landers column is published in your local newspaper, it is motivating to show students the column and encourage them to read it regularly.

TO THE STUDENT

WHAT IS THIS BOOK ABOUT?

Ann Landers' column represents a kind of journalism that has a long history in the United States. There are similar columns in newspapers around the world. People who are confused and uncertain about personal problems can write to a newspaper columnist for advice. Answers to these letters are printed in the daily paper. Because the situations are so human, most everyone enjoys reading the person's letter and the columnist's answer.

This book includes a selection of letters sent to Ann Landers, one of the best-known of the many advice columnists. All of these letters are real; they were written by ordinary Americans and published in newspapers across the country. The letters reflect direct and purposeful uses of English to express important events and common feelings. All end with a request for advice of some kind.

WHAT WILL YOU BE DOING?

To practice reading skills, you will read examples of everyday, informal written English. The sentences in these letters tend to be short and simple; they are not complicated by many clauses, flowery phrases, or long and lovely images. The writers are not trying to impress anyone. They are trying only to express a personal problem for which they want advice. The letters are good examples of clear, effective writing.

To practice vocabulary skills, you will learn words that are frequently used to express feelings and attitudes, as well as idioms and informal expressions often spoken but seldom written. You will use many new (and known) vocabulary words as you discuss each letter.

To practice writing skills, you will communicate your personal opinions by writing answers to the letters as if you were Ann Landers. These assignments will be short and will give you the opportunity to express your own beliefs and values about particular social or personal problems. The letters which you write will be circulated and read by your classmates. You can decide whether you want to use a "pen name" or your own name.

To practice speaking skills, you will participate in discussions with your classmates and express different facts and feelings in paired practice. You will role-play, too, by taking the part of someone and saying what you think is appropriate to the situation. In this way, you will practice expressing emotions such as anger, blame, surprise, sympathy, or embarrassment. This will increase your confidence in speaking and understanding conversational English.

In conclusion, here is what a foreign student of English recently wrote to Ann Landers. The letter was published in papers all over the country in May 1980.

> **Dear Ann Landers,**
> I am a foreign student who has been in this country four years. Soon I will be leaving for home and wanted to let you know how much you have helped me. I learned not only about the English language from you but about human nature.
> Your writing is one of the things I will miss most when I leave the United States.
> **A Foreign Friend**

And Ann Landers' reply:

> **Dear Friend,**
> Sorry you didn't tell me where you are going. My column appears in many foreign countries in the English language newspapers. Maybe you can continue to read me. I hope so. Bon voyage and God bless.

ACKNOWLEDGEMENTS

I would like to thank the following colleagues, students, and friends who at one time or another participated in the development of this material: the students in the *programme intensif* at the TESL Centre, Concordia University, Montreal; the students and teachers in the International Students Program at Saint Michael's College, Winooski, Vermont; Virginia Wright Lezhnev, Western Kentucky University, Bowling Green, Kentucky; John Haskell, Northeastern Illinois University; and Joan Gonzalez, University of Puerto Rico, Mayaguez.

I am pleased to acknowledge the Field Newspaper Syndicate in Chicago and Ann Landers' kind permission to reprint this selection of letters from her column. I am especially grateful to Deborah Kaufman and the Addison-Wesley editorial staff for their professional assistance and advice.

Finally, I extend special thanks to Donald Knapp, who sacrificed precious time from his garden to give me the benefit of his insight and experience. And extra special thanks to Jacqueline Flamm and Leland Northam, who provided both the push and the pull.

Richard Yorkey
August, 1980

1

TV or not TV?

Dear Ann Landers,
Ron is 21 and I am 19. We're newlyweds, and our problem is the TV in the bedroom. Ron likes to lie in bed and watch TV until midnight every night and some nights he watches until 1 AM.

I want to turn off the TV at 11 PM because I have to get up at seven for work, and if I don't get eight hours sleep I am very crabby the next morning. Ron gets up at seven too, but he says he doesn't need as much sleep as I do. Anyway, I can't fall asleep while the TV is on, and Ron refuses to turn it off at 11 PM.

How can this problem be solved? Don't suggest ear plugs because they hurt my ears.

Crabby

FACTUAL QUESTIONS
1. What does Ron like to do every night?
2. What does his wife want to do?
3. How many hours of sleep does his wife need?
4. What happens if she doesn't get this much sleep?
5. Does Ron need as much sleep as his wife?
6. Why can't his wife wear ear plugs?

DISCUSSION
1. What does the writer want Ann Landers to tell her to do?
2. What kind of relationship do you think the writer and her husband have?
3. Is Ron willing to compromise? Is Crabby?
4. How do you think this problem can be solved?

VOCABULARY
newlyweds
crabby

LANGUAGE IN LIFE

★ With a partner, role-play the following conversation between Ron and his wife at 11:00 PM. Be kind and considerate to each other. Listen to your partner's desires, but politely insist on your own desire.

Crabby	*Ron*
1. Politely ask Ron to turn off the TV.	1. Politely express desire to keep TV on.
2. Politely explain need for sleep.	2. Politely express desire to see a particular TV show.
3. Politely suggest a compromise: TV on tonight but off tomorrow night.	3. Politely express agreement.

★★ With a partner, role-play the following conversation between Ron and his wife at 11:00 PM. Now you are angry with your husband/wife. If you're Ron, be determined to leave the TV on. If you're Crabby, be equally determined to turn the TV off.

Crabby	*Ron*
1. Demand that Ron turn the TV off.	1. Refuse to do so.
2. Demand to know why he won't turn it off.	2. Explain that you want to see a special show that is on only this night.
3. Express displeasure. Explain you need eight hours sleep or you'll be crabby.	3. Express sarcastic agreement; she has seemed more and more crabby lately.

WRITING

Write a reply to Crabby, as if you were Ann Landers, and suggest a solution to her problem.

from the desk of ANN LANDERS

Dear Crabby,
You have two choices: separate rooms or a 50–50 compromise. (Turn the TV off at 11:00 every *other* night.) But remember: although a compromise makes a good umbrella, it's a poor roof.

DISCUSSION

1. Do you think that Ron will agree to such a compromise? What will happen if there are TV programs which he wants to watch on two consecutive nights?
2. Explain what Ann Landers means when she says, "although a compromise makes a good umbrella, it's a poor roof."

LANGUAGE IN LIFE

★ Who has a problem? Ron? Crabby? Both of them? Talk with a partner about what you think Ron and Crabby should do to solve their problem.

★★ Assume that Ron and Crabby can't agree on a 50–50 compromise. Crabby decides to sleep in another room. Choose a partner and prepare and present a brief dialogue which dramatizes Crabby's decision and Ron's response.

WRITING

1. Does a member of your family have a habit that annoys you or makes you crabby? Write about it. What have you tried to do about it?
2. Be honest: Do you think *you* have a habit that annoys someone in your family? What is it? How does the other family member behave when you do it?

2

Male Mixes Up Mail

Dear Ann Landers,
Don't chew me out. Just tell me what to do. I have two "best" girls, one in the Midwest, another here in town. The in-town girl is visiting relatives on the West Coast.
I wrote to them both last night. It was late and I was tired. After I wrote the letters, I decided to walk to the corner and drop them in the mailbox.

This morning I have a terrible feeling that I put the letter to the blonde in the envelope addressed to the redhead. The redhead is really Numero Uno and if she receives the blonde's letter, I am in real trouble. Can you think of something I can do before the bomb drops?

Dunderhead

FACTUAL QUESTIONS
1. How many "best" girls does the writer have?
2. Where does each one live?
3. Why did he write to the girl who lives in his hometown?
4. What did he do after he wrote the letters?
5. What does he think may have happened?

LANGUAGE USE
1. What is the style of this letter? Direct? Casual? Why would the writer use this style?
2. How old do you think the letter writer is? What expressions does he use that support this?

DISCUSSION
1. What does the writer want Ann Landers to tell him?
2. What is the writer really worried about? Losing both girl friends? Looking stupid?
3. What do you think the boy will do if "the bomb drops"?
4. What suggestions do you have for Dunderhead—in case the bomb does drop?
5. What is the obvious way to avoid this kind of mistake?
6. What kind of person do you think Dunderhead is? Would you want him as a friend? A boyfriend?

VOCABULARY
to chew someone out
Numero Uno
a dunderhead

LANGUAGE IN LIFE

★ Assume that Dunderhead did not, in fact, mix up the letters: the in-town girl received the letter that he intended for her. But he still is not sure when he meets her after she returns from the West Coast. Give the characters names and role-play their conversation.

Dunderhead	*In-town Girl*
1. Welcome her back with uncertain enthusiasm.	1. Return his greeting; say how good it is to be back.
2. Ask if she had a good time.	2. Reply affirmatively with excitement. Tell about going to Disneyland and Universal City where Hollywood movies are made.
3. Respond to her excitement about Disneyland and Hollywood. Then hesitantly ask if she received your letter.	3. Reply affirmatively and thank him with a comment about the contents.
4. As she continues to talk, smile with a sense of relief.	4. Continue describing Disneyland and Hollywood with great enthusiasm.

★★ Assume that Dunderhead *did* mix up the letters. The in-town girl received the letter that he wrote to the Midwest girl. When his in-town girl returns, however, Dunderhead still doesn't know if "the bomb is going to drop." Give the characters names and role-play their conversation.

Dunderhead	*In-town Girl*
1. Welcome her back with uncertain enthusiasm.	1. Return his greeting somewhat coldly.
2. Ask if she had a good time.	2. Briefly respond affirmatively.
3. Tell her how glad you are to see her again.	3. Question his sincerity.
4. Pretend you don't understand why she doubts you.	4. Challenge his lack of understanding. Tell him you received the letter he wrote to another girl.
5. Make up a story to explain why you wrote to the other girl. Assure this girl that she is really Numero Uno.	5. Reply any way you like.

WRITING
Now, as if you were Ann Landers, write a reply to Dunderhead.

from the desk of **ANN LANDERS**

Dear Dunderhead,
   Sorry, I can't think of a thing. Next time don't write to anybody when you're tired. And make it a rule never to mail a letter until you've let it sit overnight.

DISCUSSION
1. Do you feel that Ann Landers' reply will disappoint Dunderhead? Why? What kind of advice did he want?
2. Can *you* think of something that Dunderhead might do?

WRITING
A. Assume that you have mixed up two letters in the same way as Dunderhead. The first envelope, addressed to your best friend, should contain a letter in which you have written a very detailed account of your first date with a new girl/boy. The second envelope, addressed to your old girl/boyfriend, should contain a letter explaining why you can't come visit that weekend. Write both letters.
B. Using Dunderhead's letter as a model, write a letter to Ann Landers asking for advice. Assume that you have mixed up two letters in the same way as Dunderhead. Decide what their contents might be. (For example, Letter 1 might be a highly personal letter about your spouse, written to a very close friend. Letter 2 might be a thank-you note to your gossipy neighbors for their contributions to a local charity.) Write Ann Landers for advice. Assume that you are a middle-aged, middle-class citizen. Use a formal style of writing that contrasts with the informal style of Dunderhead.

3

Shoplifting Causes Sleepless Nights

Dear Ann Landers,
I'm not a teenager, I'm a grown woman who should have known better—but I didn't. Two weeks ago I shoplifted a $55 leather purse from a department store. I got away with it, but I haven't had a good night's sleep since.

I hate what I did and I hate the purse. I'll never carry it.

I want to return it but I'm afraid I may be arrested or told never to come into the store again. I've been told that cash gets ripped off in post offices a lot these days, so I'm afraid to send the money. Please suggest a solution.

Guilt-Ridden

FACTUAL QUESTIONS
1. How old is the woman?
2. What did she do?
3. How does she feel about it now?
4. Why is she afraid to return the purse?
5. Why is she afraid to send the money?

DISCUSSION
1. How could the woman return the purse to the store without being identified?
2. If she is afraid to send cash through the mail, why can't she send a personal check?
3. Have you ever done something which you knew was wrong and later felt guilty about it? Describe what you did and how you felt.
4. What does "I'm not a teenager, I'm a grown woman who should have known better" imply?
5. The woman says that she hates the purse and will never carry it. Why, then, did she take it in the first place?

VOCABULARY
to shoplift
leather
a purse
to get away with something
to rip off, to get ripped off
guilt-ridden

WRITING
Write a reply to Guilt-Ridden, as if you were Ann Landers, and suggest a solution to her problem.

VOCABULARY

a cashier's check
an apology
anonymous

Dear Guilt-Ridden,
  Have a cashier's check, in the amount of $55.00, made out at a bank. Request that your name not appear. Send the check to the store with a note of explanation and apology—anonymous, of course. You'll sleep better the minute the check is in the mail.

LANGUAGE IN LIFE
In English, you can make or offer an apology. To apologize, you can say:

(Please) (I hope you'll)	excuse pardon forgive	me for (not) doing something . . .

or: I'm (very) sorry that . . .

Often an apology is followed by an explanation. For example:
(You bump into someone) "Oh, I'm sorry. I didn't see you."
(You miss an appointment) "Please forgive me. I thought the meeting was on Thursday, not Tuesday."
(You arrive late) "I hope you'll excuse me for being late. The traffic was unusually heavy this morning."

How you accept or refuse an apology depends on the seriousness of the offense. In most cases, a simple "Thank you," "Don't worry," "That's all right," or "Forget it" is sufficient.

★ Practice in pairs. A apologizes to B. B politely accepts A's apology.
1. You accidentally step on B's toe.
2. You arrive late for an appointment.
3. You mispronounce B's name.
4. You return a borrowed book with several torn pages.
5. You have forgotten B's name.
6. Coming around a corner, you bump into B.
7. You interrupt a conversation to ask what time it is.
8. You misunderstand B. He said $50.00 but you thought he said $15.00.
9. During a formal dinner, you spill your glass of wine.
10. You cannot pay back until next week the $10.00 that you borrowed from B.

WRITING

Assume you are "Guilt-Ridden" and you have read Ann Landers' reply. Write the anonymous "note of explanation and apology" that she advises.

4

Embarrassed to Ask

LETTER 4-A

 **DEAR ANN LANDERS,**
I'm 16, a high school sophomore who enjoys knitting. I've made myself some pretty sweaters. A teacher complimented me on one of my creations and asked if I'd make one for her. She offered to pay me.

I was thrilled, bought the yarn the next day and had her sweater ready within a week. When I handed it to her, she said, "Thank you. It's lovely"—and not one word about paying me. What should I do?

Knit-Wit

VOCABULARY

to be embarrassed
a sophomore
to knit
to compliment
  someone
yarn
a "knit-wit" (compare
  this with "nitwit")

FACTUAL QUESTIONS

1. Who is the writer of this letter?
2. How old is the writer?
3. What does the writer enjoy doing?
4. Why did the teacher compliment the student?
5. What did the teacher ask the student to do?
6. Did the teacher offer to pay the student?
7. Did the teacher pay the student?
8. What does the student want to know?

LETTER 4-B

DEAR ANN LANDERS,
I am 12 years old, but my problem is just as serious as any grown-up's. Our neighbors asked me if I would feed their dogs, collect their mail and newspapers, and water their plants while they were away on a two-week vacation. They said they would pay me when they came home.

I had the papers and mail ready for them in a neat pile. The dogs were in great shape, and the plants looked better than when they left. I got a "thank you" and a lot of compliments, but not one word was said about the pay.

I was counting on the money to help me buy my dad a nice birthday gift. Please tell me what to do.

Disappointed in Bakersfield

FACTUAL QUESTIONS

1. How old is the writer?
2. What was the writer asked to do?
3. How long were the neighbors going to be away?
4. Did the neighbors promise to pay for the work?
5. What had the writer done with the papers and the mail?
6. What did the writer get instead of money?
7. What was the writer going to do with the money?
8. What does the writer want to know?

VOCABULARY
neat
a pile
to count on something

CULTURAL NOTES

1. Reread each of these letters carefully. Are there any clues that help you tell whether the writers are male or female?
2. People in some cultures would say that the writer of Letter 4-A is female, and the writer of Letter 4-B is male. Why? What do you think?
3. A *stereotype* refers to a fixed pattern of behavior which is believed to be representative of a type of person or a group of people. For example, in the United States, a common cultural stereotype is that knitting is something which only females do. Few males are seen with knitting needles and yarn. What is the attitude in your country? Look at the photo of Rosie Grier. What is he doing?

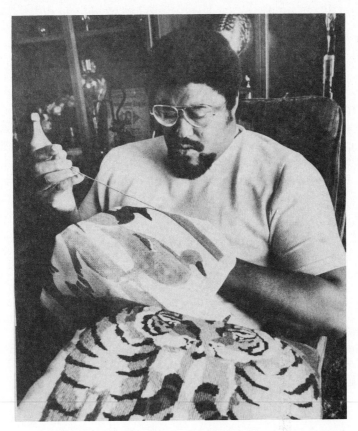

"This is Roosevelt Grier, a famous American football player . . ."

4. What kinds of jobs is the writer of the second letter doing? Are these the kinds of jobs that young boys or girls usually do? What about in the country you come from?
5. How much money do these jobs pay? Is there another value in doing such work?

21

DISCUSSION

1. What advice does the writer of 4-A want from Ann Landers?
2. Has a situation of this kind ever happened to you? If so, how did you handle it?
3. In Letter 4-A, do you think that the student may have misunderstood? Do you think that the teacher deliberately did not pay the student, or simply forgot? What do you think of people who don't do things they've agreed or promised to do?
4. Do you think the student should have agreed to make a sweater for the teacher? Why or why not? How friendly do you think teachers and students should be? Explain.
5. In Letter 4-B, do you think the boy/girl may have misunderstood, or did the neighbors forget, deliberately or not?
6. In a situation like this, is it better to confront the person directly, approach the person indirectly, or simply forget about it? What would *you* do?

LANGUAGE IN LIFE

It is often embarrassing to have to ask someone for money that they have agreed but neglected to pay. It is especially difficult for a young person to ask an adult, or for a student to ask a teacher. Rather than *demand* payment, is is first more polite to *request* it, recognizing the possibility of a genuine misunderstanding. Possible approaches are:

"*I thought that* you were going to pay me for my work."
"*I understood that* you agreed to pay me for the sweater."
"*It was my impression that* you agreed to pay me for my work."

What other things could you say?

It is sometimes a good idea to provide a diplomatic excuse for the person in case a graceful explanation is needed. This allows the person to "save face." For example:

"Perhaps you were so busy at the time that you forgot about your agreement to pay me for the sweater."
"Maybe you were so excited about your vacation that you don't remember agreeing to pay me for my two-weeks' work."

What other "face-saving" devices could you use?

★ Choose the situation described in either Letter 4-A or 4-B. With a partner, decide on names and role-play the following conversation.

A	B
1. Ask if your work was satisfactory.	1. Reply affirmatively, express thanks and add praise.
2. Thank B. Politely state that you expected to be paid. Politely remind B that you have not been paid.	2. Express genuine surprise at having forgotten. Apologize for the oversight. Agree to pay immediately.
3. Thank B graciously.	3. Thank A for reminding you and for being so polite about it.

★★ Choose the situation described in either Letter 4-A or 4-B. With a partner decide on names and role-play the following conversation.

A	B
1. Ask if your work was satisfactory.	1. Reply affirmatively, express thanks and add praise.
2. Thank B, but politely remind B that he/she agreed to pay you.	2. Express genuine surpise at the idea. State that you don't recall at all any agreement to pay.
3. Explain the circumstances in detail, as you remember the agreement to pay.	3. Disagree. Explain that you had the impression that A agreed to do the work voluntarily.
4. Try to correct this wrong impression politely.	4. Agree to pay for the work—even though you don't recall any such agreement—because you are pleased with the work.

WRITING

Now, as if you were Ann Landers, write a reply to either Letter 4-A or 4-B.

from the desk of ANN LANDERS

Dear Knit-Wit,

Send her a bill for the cost of the yarn and add $20 for labor. Next time someone says, "I'll pay you," discuss the price openly, settle on a figure, write it down and behave in a business-like manner.

Dear Bakersfield,

It's a little late to be talking about money, but do it anyway. Simply say, "You offered to pay me for taking care of the mail and papers, the dogs and the plants. I would like the money now, please."

And let this be a lesson to you, son. When you go into any kind of a business deal, settle on the amount and the time of payment *before* you perform the service. If you want to be extra business-like, write the agreement on a piece of paper and ask, "Is this right?" Then ask for a signature.

DISCUSSION

1. Does Ann Landers show any stereotypical thinking in her reply to Bakersfield?
2. Do you agree with her advice to Knit-Wit and Bakersfield? Why or why not?

WRITING

Work in pairs. Ask your partner what you can do for him while he's away on a trip. Ask how much he's willing to pay you. List all the work you're willing to do, and come to an agreement about the amount of money. When you're both happy with your "business deal," put both your signatures on it. Change roles and make a new agreement. Share/compare your written agreements with the rest of the class. Note: Often payments to friends will not be in money, but may take the form of "payment in kind." What does this mean? Are you and your partner more comfortable with this kind of arrangement?

5

Hippy Father; Unhappy Son

Dear Ann Landers,
I am a 17-year-old boy with a problem. My father is 51. He and my mom are separated, so Dad moved into a singles apartment, and now he is a changed person. He let his hair grow long, he wears strange clothes and beads, and he doesn't even look like my father any more.

The majority of the people who live in the building are in their 20's and 30's, and my father must think he fits right in with them, which he doesn't. People must think he is going through his second childhood.

I want to tell him how stupid he looks, but I don't want to hurt him. How can I put it to him gently that he is making a fool of himself?

Embarrassed

FACTUAL QUESTIONS
1. Why did the boy's father move out of the house?
2. In what way is his father now a changed person?
3. What does the boy suppose his father must think?
4. What does he suppose his father's neighbors must think?
5. What does the boy want to tell his father?
6. What does he ask Ann Landers?

VOCABULARY
hippy
a singles apartment
beads
a majority
embarrassed

CULTURAL NOTES
1. What do you think a singles apartment is? Who probably lives there? Are there any singles apartments in your area?
2. What does "He and my mom are separated" mean?

DISCUSSION

1. Where do you suppose the son is living now, with his mother or his father? Why do you suppose so?
2. Many 17-year-old boys let their hair grow long and wear tee shirts, leather vests, beads, blue jeans and sandals. Do you suppose this boy does?
3. Why is the boy embarrassed? For himself? For his father?
4. Although he is embarrassed by his father's clothes and behavior, do you think he still loves his father?
5. What does it mean to "go through a second childhood"? (Clue: How is his father acting?)
6. Do you have any friends who embarrass you by their clothing or life-style? What would you say to them?

LANGUAGE IN LIFE

★ To be embarrassed is to feel ashamed, awkward, or socially uncomfortable. There are various ways in which we can express embarrassment. For example:

1. I remember being embarrassed when I thought my friend's wife was his mother.
2. One time my boyfriend embarrassed me by kissing me in public, right in the middle of the street.
3. The worst embarrassment, I think, is to forget the name of your date.

Use one of these patterns and describe an embarrassing moment that you have had.

★★ Assume that the 51-year-old man and the 17-year-old boy have a heart-to-heart, father-and-son talk. With a partner role-play the following conversation.

Son	*Father*
1. Express love and respect for your father, but express embarrassment at his dress and behavior.	1. Express surprise and request explanation.
2. Explain difference between your father's age and his clothes and life-style.	2. Express disagreement. Express need to be yourself.
3. Ask if this need is right when it embarrasses you.	3. Express regret, but insist on being yourself.

WRITING

Now write a reply that answers the question at the end of the boy's letter.

VOCABULARY
life-style
to suit himself

from the desk of **ANN LANDERS**

Dear Embarrassed,
Underneath the long hair, beads and those "strange clothes," he's still your father. There is no way to tell him "gently" that you think he's making a fool of himself. He has the right to change his life-style to suit himself, and it's not your place to judge him.

DISCUSSION
1. Do you agree that it's not a son's place to judge his father?
2. If the father "has the right to change his life-style to suit himself," doesn't the son have the right to express his embarrassment?
3. The son has said he doesn't want to hurt his father. Ann Landers says there is no way to tell him gently. Should the boy speak or not speak?

WRITING
Assume you are the father of this boy. Your son has told you that your clothes and behavior embarrass him. You are hurt that your son is ashamed of you, and angry that he has judged you so badly. You do not know that he wrote to Ann Landers. You write a letter to Ann Landers, explaining the situation from your viewpoint. Ask for her advice.

6

An Uninvited Guest

Dear Ann Landers,

What should a person do if he is dining in the home of a friend and he comes upon a foreign substance in the food like, shall we say, a hairpin in the soufflé? This happened to me recently and I said nothing, but it could have been a serious thing.

Yesterday I had a similar experience, only it was a worm in a fresh peach which had been sliced and served over ice cream. I was speaking to the hostess when I noticed it. I kept my wits about me, continued to talk, and ate around the worm.

If such a thing happens again, what should be done? Do you feel the hostess would want to know?

Lost My Appetite

FACTUAL QUESTIONS
1. What recently happened to this letter writer?
2. What was the similar experience yesterday?
3. What did the writer do about it?
4. What is the question that the writer asks?

DISCUSSION

VOCABULARY
to come upon
a foreign substance
shall we say
a soufflé
a worm
to slice
a hostess
kept my wits about
    me
appetite

1. Is the writer a man or a woman? What evidence do you have for your answer?
2. Have you ever had this kind of experience? If so, describe the circumstances and what you did.
3. If you were the host or hostess, would you expect or want your guests to tell you if anything is wrong with the food that you serve?
4. Would you act differently if this happened in a restaurant? Why?
5. What would you do in a similar situation if you didn't like the food your hostess had prepared?

LANGUAGE IN LIFE

★ Suppose you decide that the answer to the question in the last sentence is: Yes, the hostess would want to know. You might say, "Excuse me, there seems to be a worm in my peach." Suggest other polite ways to tell your hostess this embarrassing information.

★★ Suppose this happens in a very expensive restaurant and you are extremely upset. Demand that the management pay for your meal, which has been ruined.

WRITING

Write a letter, as if you were Ann Landers, that answers the question asked by Lost My Appetite.

from the desk of **ANN LANDERS**

Dear Lost,
Anyone who can eat around a worm and carry on a conversation with the hostess at the same time doesn't need advice from Ann Landers. I don't think the hostess would "want to know." Keep quiet, honey.

DISCUSSION

1. Do you agree or disagree with Ann Landers' advice?
2. Do you think that the answer to the question, "Do you feel the hostess would want to know?", depends on how well the hostess and guest know each other?
3. If the guest eats around the worm, he or she presumably would leave the worm on the plate. In this case, the hostess is likely to see the worm later. Then how do you suppose she will feel?

7

Picking Up the Pieces

Dear Ann Landers,
I have had the same cleaning woman for ten years. If she had one more brain she would be an imbecile. I don't know why I've put up with her for so long. Maybe I'm the imbecile. Please don't tell me to let her go. I can't do it. She has five children and needs this job. Also, when I was in the hospital, she was here every morning at 7:30 through snowstorms and blizzards.

Problem: Yesterday she tried to vacuum the carpeting on the stairs with the large sweeper because she was too lazy to use the small attachment. The sweeper got out of control, fell down the stairs, and broke into 20 pieces. The repair bill was $48.

Should I make her pay for it? Answer Yes or No.

Mad in Missouri

VOCABULARY
an imbecile
to put up with
   someone or
   something
to let someone go
a blizzard
to vacuum
carpeting
a sweeper
an attachment

FACTUAL QUESTIONS
1. Why does the writer think the cleaning woman is stupid? Does she give any evidence?
2. If she thinks the cleaning woman is not good, why hasn't she dismissed her?
3. Exactly what did the cleaning woman do that made the writer so mad?
4. What is the writer's question?

CULTURAL NOTE
A *cleaning woman* (sometimes a *cleaning lady*) is hired, usually by the hour, to clean private homes and offices. Do you think they are as common in private homes now as they were in the past?

LANGUAGE USE

Sarcasm is language intended to hurt someone's feelings; it is often satirical or ironic. Note the sarcasm: "If she had one more brain she would be an imbecile." What does the writer mean by this unkind statement? Does she demonstrate the woman's stupidity or just complain of her laziness? Is sarcasm appropriate or effective in this letter? In any situation?

DISCUSSION

1. The writer has had this cleaning woman for ten years. If she really is so stupid and lazy, why do you suppose she has put up with her for so long?
2. Should an employee be responsible for the tools and equipment which the employer provides?
3. The writer wants a plain answer, yes or no. Are you willing to be so definite? Is there the possibility of an answer in between?
4. What do you think the writer wants Ann Landers to tell her to do?

LANGUAGE IN LIFE

★ When you pardon someone's wrong thoughts or actions, you express forgiveness. In formal English, you might say or write, "I forgive you for . . ." or "This time I am willing to overlook . . ." However, in informal conversation you are more likely to say "That's all right" or "It doesn't matter." For example, the writer of this letter might say to the cleaning woman, "You really shouldn't have been so careless. But it doesn't matter; the vacuum cleaner can be repaired. Next time, however, try to be more careful."

Informally express forgiveness to someone who:
1. spills coffee on your homework paper;
2. arrives late for an appointment;
3. telephones at midnight and awakens you;
4. steps on your toe in a crowded elevator;
5. returns a borrowed book very late;
6. breaks a cheap glass ashtray.

★★ When the writer saw the twenty broken pieces of the vacuum cleaner, she might have told the cleaning woman:

That was a | careless / stupid / brilliant | thing to do.

All three statements express a judgment, but they show different degrees of anger. "That was a careless thing to do" implies the least criticism and anger. "That was a stupid thing to do" says that the woman was not only careless but unthinking and foolish as well. "That was a brilliant thing to do" is an example of *sarcasm*.

Sarcasm is an unkind use of language; it is wise to use it carefully, if at all. However, you ought to be able to recognize it when you hear it. The following exercise illustrates how sarcasm is sometimes used. For example:

1. You and a friend agreed to meet at 2:00. Your friend keeps you waiting until 2:30.
   You might say, "Thanks so much for being here on time."
2. You read a book which you think was very dull. It bored you.
   You might tell someone, "That was the most exciting book I've read since the telephone book."

Now think of sarcastic comments for the following situations:

3. Your friend tells a joke that is not at all funny.
4. Your friend is wearing some article of clothing (hat, dress, necktie, coat, shoes, etc.) which you think is unnecessarily expensive, very unattractive, and completely ridiculous.
5. You see a movie which is so boring that you keep falling asleep.
6. You eat at a restaurant that serves terrible food.
7. Your friend thinks that he or she is good looking enough to become a popular movie star.
8. Your friend thinks that he or she is a great singer and insists on demonstrating.
9. Your friend thinks that he or she is the world's greatest driver.
10. You think this exercise is the least useful in the book.

WRITING
Write a letter to Mad in Missouri, as if you were Ann Landers, and answer the question, "Should I make her pay for it?"

VOCABULARY
now and then
it's your turn

---

from the desk of **ANN LANDERS**

Dear Mad,
   No. Even some smart people do stupid things now and then. From your description, the woman gave *you* special consideration and now it's your turn.

DISCUSSION

1. Do you agree with Ann Landers' advice? Does it seem to be fair? Do you feel that there may be some sarcasm in her answer?
2. Suppose the woman had omitted the information about the cleaning woman being so considerate and helpful. Would this have made any difference, do you think, in Ann Landers' reply?

8

Lover's Language Worries Lover

Dear Ann Landers,
I have been dating a young man for several years. Dan is everything a girl could want. Well, almost. He is kind, nice looking, considerate, fun to be with, and he makes good money. The only drawback is his grammer. For example, he says "I seen," "youse," "have went," and "between you and I."

I bite my tongue when he makes these awful mistakes, especially in the presence of my friends. I don't want to be ashamed of him, Ann, and I don't want to embarrass him either, but I'm afraid one day I might.

Is there a chance that we can have a good marriage in spite of this? I am 26 and a college graduate. Dan is 27 and attended a trade school. I do love him, but I fear I'll be a nagging wife—or worse yet, a silent wife who is ashamed of her husband's grammer.

Please hurry your answer. He is waiting for mine.

York, Pennsylvania

VOCABULARY
considerate
a drawback
to bite one's tongue
to be ashamed
to embarrass
a trade school
to nag
in spite of

FACTUAL QUESTIONS
1. How long have she and Dan been dating?
2. Why does she like Dan?
3. What is the drawback?
4. What doesn't she want to do?
5. What is she afraid of?
6. What question does she ask Ann Landers?

LANGUAGE USE
Note the last line of the letter. *Mine* is a possessive pronoun. In this case, what does it take the place of? What question is Dan asking the girl?

DISCUSSION

1. Have you ever been embarrassed by someone's bad grammar? Are there mistakes in your own language similar to the kinds that upset this girl? Are some kinds of mistakes in your language considered to be more serious than other kinds of mistakes?
2. Do you think that speaking or writing your own language incorrectly can be a drawback in work or business, in social situations, or in a marriage? Explain.
3. How, or by whom, is correctness in your language decided? Do you believe that anything a native speaker says is acceptable, even if it doesn't follow the traditional rules?
4. When you make a mistake while speaking English in class, how do you feel about your teacher correcting you? Would you rather be corrected (1) immediately, (2) after you have finished what you wanted to say, or (3) alone in private? Why?
5. When you're talking with an English-speaking friend, how do you feel about being corrected if you make a mistake?
6. The writer of this letter is a college graduate. The man she wants to marry is not. Do you think this difference in education makes a difference in the success of a marriage? If only one person of a married couple can be college educated, does it matter if it's the husband or the wife? Why? What difference does it make?

LANGUAGE IN LIFE

There are levels of politeness which we use to disagree with others about something. For example:

LESS
POLITE

"You don't know what you're talking about!"
"No, no, no! You're wrong!"
"I'm sorry but you're wrong."
"Pardon me, but I think you're mistaken."
"Excuse me, but I believe that you're mistaken."

MORE
POLITE

There are also several levels of politeness to correct someone. For example:

LESS
POLITE

"Excuse me, X, but the past tense of *see* is *saw*."
"Excuse me, X, may I correct your grammar? The past tense of *see* is *saw*."
"Pardon me, X, do you mind if I correct your grammar? The past tense of *see* is *saw*, I think, not *seen*."

MORE
POLITE

★1. Assume that Dan has made the following mistakes. Politely correct him.
1. Yesterday I seen him.
2. All of youse are invited.
3. I've went to three Yankee baseball games this week.
4. This is a secret just between you and I.
5. It was a boring weekend. I didn't do nothing at all.

★2. Politely correct a student who makes one of the following mistakes.

Mistake	Correction
1. spells *pronounciation*	*pronunciation*
2. spells *fourty*	*forty*
3. spells *wich*	*which*
4. spells *untill*	*until*
5. spells *occured*	*occurred*
6. pronounces *said* (rhymes with *paid*)	*said* (rhymes with *dead*)
7. pronounces *live* (like *leave*)	*live* (rhymes with *give*)
8. pronounces DIS-*tri-bute*	dis-TRI-*bute*
9. pronounces *women* (like *woman*)	*women* (rhymes with *swimmin'*)

★3. Work in pairs. Take turns politely correcting each other.

Statement	Correction
1. Columbus discovered America in 1592.	1492
2. Texas is the largest state in the United States.	Alaska
3. Michaelangelo painted The Last Supper.	Leonardo da Vinci
4. Elvis Presley died in 1975.	1977
5. Quito is the capital of Peru.	Ecuador
6. Saturn is the largest planet in the solar system.	Jupiter
7. Mach 1 refers to the speed of light.	sound
8. It was Marc Antony who assassinated Julius Caesar.	Brutus

★★ Statements of opinion can be politely challenged in much the same way as statements of fact. The only difference is that neither person is necessarily right or wrong. The level of politeness depends on how well the other person is known. Forms that are more polite are used in situations that are more formal. For this activity, work in threes. After Student 1 states a personal opinion, Student 2 should counter it with an opinion of his or her own. Student 3 should counter Student 2's opinion and offer one of his or her own. Use different levels of politeness.

Student 1	Student 2	Student 3
1. Joe Louis was the greatest boxer of all time.	Jack Dempsey	Muhammad Ali
2. Paris is the most exciting city in the world.	New York	Rio de Janeiro
3. The best group of musical entertainers is Kiss.	Fleetwood Mac	Pink Floyd
4. _____ is the easiest language to learn.	_____	_____
5. The friendliest people in the world live in _____ .	_____	_____
6. _____ is the best popular singer today.	_____	_____
7. The most beautiful sounding word in English is _____ .	_____	_____
8. The funniest joke I ever heard is _____ .	_____	_____

WRITING

Now write a reply to York's letter, as if you were Ann Landers.

from the desk of **ANN LANDERS**

Dear York,
Dan sounds too good to discard. Ask him if he wants to be corrected—when the two of you are alone, of course.

Incidentally, you misspelled the word grammar throughout your letter. It is *ar*, dear. Perhaps you and Dan are not as far apart as you think.

VOCABULARY
to discard
incidentally

DISCUSSION

1. Do you agree with Ann Landers that Dan is too good to discard? Why or why not? If Dan and York get married, what kind of relationship do you think they will have?
2. What if Dan tells York he doesn't *want* to be corrected, that he thinks his English is fine? What should she do? What would *you* do?
3. What things/qualities are most important to a successful marriage, in your opinion? What kind of man or woman is your ideal mate? How would he or she talk, behave, dress, feel, think?

9

Dieting Diners Hurt Hostess

Dear Ann Landers,
I had a dinner party recently and invited five couples. I worked hard because I wanted everything to be just right.

Two of my guests brought their own "dinner" in a jar. It was some kind of diet concoction. I was angry and thought they had a lot of nerve accepting my dinner invitation when they knew they weren't going to eat anything. I told them how hard I had worked preparing the dinner and urged them to "fall off the wagon" for just that meal, but they wouldn't do it.

I finally decided to be a good sport, but deep down I was hurt. What do you think of such guests, and how would you have handled it?

Still Burning

FACTUAL QUESTIONS
1. How many people were invited to the writer's dinner party?
2. What did two of the guests bring? Why?
3. How did the writer feel?
4. What did she try to do first?
5. What question does she ask Ann Landers?

VOCABULARY
a jar
diet
a concoction
to have a lot of nerve
to fall off the wagon
a good sport
Still Burning

LANGUAGE USE
1. The writer encloses the word *dinner* within quotation marks. Why does she do this? How does she feel about her guests' diet concoction?
2. The original idiom "to be on the (water) wagon" means to refrain from drinking alcoholic beverages. In this letter, the idiom has been extended. Why are the two guests "on the wagon"? What are they refraining from? What does their hostess urge them to do?

DISCUSSION

1. Was it fair or polite of the hostess to encourage her guests to give up their diet especially for her dinner?
2. The writer says she was "a good sport." What does she mean? When are you a good sport?
3. The writer admits that she was angry and hurt. Apparently her anger continued, since she signed her letter "Still Burning." Do you think her anger was justified?
4. Assume that there are certain foods which, for health or religious reasons, you can't eat. What should you do if you are invited to someone's home for dinner?

LANGUAGE IN LIFE

To persuade means to get someone to do something by urging, or by arguing or reasoning with them. In a social situation, persuasion is usually expressed by a question rather than a direct statement. For example:

"Why don't you fall off the wagon just this once?" instead of
"I urge you to fall off the wagon just this once."

Any of the following questions or their variations might be used:

Would you please		
Couldn't you (please)		
Would you be willing to	fall	
Why don't you		off the wagon just this once?
Would you mind		
How about	falling	
What about		

The request is usually followed by a reason or explanation. Often the person who is asking tries to make the other feel guilty.

"Wouldn't you be willing to fall off the wagon just this once? I went to so much trouble to prepare something special for you."
"How about falling off the wagon just this once? Surely just one meal won't hurt your diet too much."

★ With a partner, prepare to role-play the following conversation:

A	B
1. Greet your guest.	1. Return the greeting.
2. Ask what is in the jar.	2. Explain you are on a diet. Apologize that you cannot eat anything but your special concoction.
3. State how hard you have worked, and that you have prepared a very special meal. Try to persuade B to fall off the wagon for just this meal.	3. Apologize again. Emphasize how important it is to stay on your diet. Express hope that A will understand.
4. Express understanding but disappointment.	4. Reply appropriately.

★★ Divide into pairs. Try to persuade each other to do the following:

A Persuade B	B Persuade A
1. to buy an English-English dictionary instead of a bilingual dictionary.	1. to help you with your English composition.
2. to let you borrow B's expensive camera.	2. to eat pickled pigs feet.
3. to go to a movie which B really doesn't want to see.	3. to ask the teacher, on behalf of the whole class, to postpone a vocabulary test.
4. to loan you $25.00.	4. to let you use A's car tonight.
5. to change B's hair style.	5. to sing a song in A's native language during an International Evening.

from the desk of ANN LANDERS

Dear Burning,
   Guests who are on special diets should say so when they are invited out. If I were the hostess and dieters appeared with their own "dinner," I'd say nothing and permit them to "drink their dinners" as inconspicuously as possible. (I would never attempt to get them to "fall off the wagon" or make them feel guilty for sticking to their diets.)

VOCABULARY
inconspicuously
to stick to something

DISCUSSION
1. Do you think the writer will be satisfied with Ann Landers' answer? Explain.
2. Ann Landers says she wouldn't want to make her guests "feel guilty." How could she avoid this?

10

College Plans Go Up in Smoke

Dear Ann Landers,
Our 16-year-old daughter started to smoke last Christmas. It killed me to see that lovely girl with a cigarette in her mouth. I told her how I felt. Martha continued to smoke, saying "It's my life," etc. I told her if she didn't stop smoking, I wouldn't send her to college. She agreed to quit.

Last night I smelled cigarette smoke on Martha's breath. She confessed she had broken her word. Now I must make good my threat.

Martha is unusually bright and wants to teach handicapped children. I am working full-time to put her older sister through school and would do the same for Martha. My husband's salary is good, but with inflation eating us up we could never educate the girls unless I pitched in.

My theory is that if smoking is more important than college, I am a fool to work to put Martha through. Your opinion is wanted.

Freeport Woe

FACTUAL QUESTIONS
1. Who is the writer of this letter—Martha's mother or father? How do you know?
2. What was Martha doing that was so upsetting?
3. Why did Martha agree to stop smoking?
4. Why must the parent now make good the threat?
5. The writer says, "Your opinion is wanted." Opinion about what?

VOCABULARY
to quit
to break one's word
to confess
to make good
  a threat
handicapped
to put someone
  through (college)
inflation
to pitch in
woe

LANGUAGE USE
The writer says "It *killed* me to see that lovely girl with a cigarette in her mouth." This exaggeration is understandable and permissible in informal writing and speaking ("My feet are killing me!"), but formal writing should be more precise. How else could she express her distress?

DISCUSSION

1. *To bribe* is to influence someone to do something by giving favors or gifts. Do you believe it is fair of parents to bribe their children ("Be a good boy and I'll let you stay up an hour longer," or "Clean up your room and I'll give you a dollar")? Is the mother's offer of college in the same category?

2. The agreement between Martha and her mother can be expressed as affirmative statements: The mother will finance the daughter's college education; in return, the daughter will agree to stop smoking. How does this bargain reflect the values of the mother? Of Martha? Do you think the bargain is equal on both sides?

3. Do you agree with the mother's theory?

LANGUAGE IN LIFE

Displeasure is expressed by such expressions as:

I	don't like dislike	your smoking. to see you smoking. it when you smoke.
	wish you wouldn't smoke.	

Prohibition is expressed by such expressions as:

You	cannot may not must not			smoke.
	are not	allowed permitted	to	
	are prohibited from smoking.			

★ Express your displeasure of something by saying, "I wish you wouldn't _____ ."
For example:

I wish you wouldn't smoke in class.
I wish you wouldn't borrow my dictionary so often.
I wish you wouldn't always come late to class.

Express each of the following prohibitions in another way. For example:

You are prohibited from using this exit. = "You are not allowed to use this exit."

1. Children are prohibited from swimming without a lifeguard present.
2. A 15-year-old is prohibited from buying liquor.
3. Teachers are prohibited from hitting their students.
4. You are prohibited from borrowing a library book for more than two weeks at a time.
5. Drivers are prohibited from driving faster than 55 mph.

★★ Express displeasure to A about the following:

1. A often interrupts you.
2. A regularly telephones you after midnight.
3. B is driving too fast.
4. C criticizes the teacher too much.
5. D always wears a dirty coat to class.

To each person, express prohibition of the following:

1. A—stay out so late on school nights.
2. B—use a dictionary during a vocabulary test.
3. C—contribute more than one dollar towards a gift for the teacher.
4. D—park within 15 feet of a fire hydrant.
5. E—pull that fire alarm unless there is a fire.

WRITING

Write a letter to Woe, as if you were Ann Landers, in which you state your opinion.

Momma

By Mell Lazarus

VOCABULARY

to paint yourself into
   a corner
to violate
cardinal
the punishment fits
   the crime
to oppose, to be
   opposed
extremely
to damage
to withdraw
previous

Dear Woe,
   You have painted yourself into a corner
by violating two cardinal rules for
disciplining children: (1) Never over-
promise or over-threaten; and (2) Make
sure the punishment fits the crime. Now
you must go to Martha and say, "I am
opposed to your smoking because it could
be extremely damaging to your health. It
is also a filthy habit and an expensive one.
I withdraw all previous threats, however,
and leave the decision up to you."

DISCUSSION

1. What was Martha's "crime"? What sort of punishment would have "fit" this crime?
2. Do you remember being disciplined as a child? What methods did your parents use?
   Which of these will you use when you're a parent?
3. Are you opposed to young people smoking? What would you do if a younger brother
   or sister were doing something you thought was dangerous or bad for them?

11

Doesn't Care to Share

Dear Ann Landers,
Recently my husband and I had dinner at a Japanese steak house with two other couples. As is customary, we were seated around the cooking area enjoying ourselves.
We all ordered a glass of plum wine. A young woman seated nearby asked if the wine was good. I replied, "Yes." She then asked me, "May I taste yours?" I hesitated, reluctant to share my glass with her. Another woman in our group then passed *her* wine. The stranger took a sip, said, "Thank you, it's delicious," then passed the glass back.
My husband felt I was ungracious for not sharing my glass with her and told me, "Mrs. C really showed you up." Was I impolite, as my husband claims?

Mrs. X

FACTUAL QUESTIONS
1. Where did this incident take place?
2. Who asked to taste Mrs. X's plum wine?
3. Why did Mrs. X hesitate?
4. Who offered the stranger a sip of the wine?
5. What did Mr. X think about what happened?

VOCABULARY
customary
plum wine
to hesitate
reluctant
a sip
ungracious
to show someone up
impolite

CULTURAL NOTE
In many Japanese restaurants in the United States, it is possible for about eight people to sit around a large table. In the center is a heated flat surface where the food is cooked in a special Japanese way. The elaborate cooking ceremony and the close seating arrangement often result in friendly discussion among strangers. Does this occur in other restaurants?

DISCUSSION

1. Why do you suppose Mrs. X was reluctant to share her glass with the stranger?
2. What do you think Mrs. X's response would have been if Mrs. C had asked to taste her wine? Or if her own husband had asked?
3. Do you agree or disagree with Mr. X?
4. What would *you* have done in her situation?

LANGUAGE IN LIFE

★ Notice these two ways to request permission. Notice especially the affirmative and negative responses.

Do you mind if I taste your wine? (*Do you mind* = Do you care, or have any objection?)	No, of course not. No, certainly not. No, not at all. Please do.	Yes, I'm sorry. I'd prefer (that) you didn't.
May I taste your wine?	Yes, of course. Yes, certainly. By all means. Please do.	No, I'm sorry. I'd prefer (that) you didn't.

Student A asks Student B for permission to do the following. Student B replies affirmatively or negatively.

1. to borrow B's dictionary.
2. to ask B a personal question.
3. to smoke.
4. to correct B's pronunciation of your name.
5. to tell a funny story about B's friend.
6. to use B's car for an hour.
7. to read B's newspaper.
8. to have another piece of cake.

Notice the use of *let* and *permit* to request permission.

Would you let me Would you mind letting me	taste your wine?
Would you permit me Would you mind permitting me	to taste your wine?

Student A asks Student B for permission to do the same things as above. This time use only *let* or *permit*.

WRITING

Write a reply to Mrs. X, as if you were Ann Landers, and answer the question in her letter.

from the desk of ANN LANDERS

Dear Mrs. X,

Sorry, I disagree with your husband. It was extremely rude of that woman to ask for a sip of wine from your glass. You were wise to hesitate and Mrs. C was foolish to offer hers. A tactful response would have been, "The wine *is* delicious. May I order you a glass?"

VOCABULARY

rude
tactful

LANGUAGE IN LIFE

★ With a partner, prepare to role-play the following conversation:

Student A	*Student B*
1. Request permission to do something.	1. Express reluctance to permit A to do it. Give a reason.
2. Accept reason, and adjust your request for permission accordingly.	2. Express agreement and thanks.

For example:

1. Do you mind if I smoke a cigar?	1. I prefer that you don't. I'm sorry, but cigar smoke is so strong.
2. Of course. May I smoke a cigarette then?	2. By all means. I don't mind cigarettes.

12

Mother Mumbles; Daughter Grumbles

Dear Ann Landers,

In a recent column you said Doris (who gets organized by talking to herself) was perfectly sane. Now can you tell me whether my mother is?

She doesn't talk to herself, but she'll come up to me and say, "Well, I've washed the clothes, put the towels and bedsheets away, done the dishes, and now I'll weed the garden, and later I should sit myself down and write letters to the family."

Mom has been rattling on like this for years, but it seems to be happening a lot more lately. It really annoys me, especially when I'm trying to do my homework.

My brother, who is in college, says she used to do this to him but it never got on his nerves the way it does mine. Do you think our mother is crazy?

Julie

VOCABULARY

to mumble
to grumble
sane
to weed
to rattle on
to annoy
to get on one's nerves

FACTUAL QUESTIONS

1. What does Julie's mother do that is so annoying?
2. When does it especially get on Julie's nerves?
3. What question does Julie ask Ann Landers?

DISCUSSION

1. Do you ever get organized by talking to yourself? Do you know anyone who does? What is said? When?
2. What is the real purpose of the mother's talking like this?

LANGUAGE IN LIFE

★ You have surely faced this situation at some time: You have to listen to someone's boring or unnecessarily long monologue. You do not want to be impolite, but you also do not want to listen any longer. You want to politely end the "conversation." Here is a possible way to make a polite interruption:

1. Listen for the grammatical end and the final falling intonation of a sentence.
2. Quickly respond to what has just been said. You can avoid argument and further discussion by politely accepting the person's facts or feelings.
3. Politely excuse yourself.
4. Explain reason for leaving or ending conversation.

For example: Assume that someone is describing his or her illness with descriptive details of various aches, pains, medicines, and treatment. After several minutes of uninterrupted talk, he or she says, ". . . and would you believe that not one of all those doctors in that hospital has . . .

1. . . . been able to tell me exactly what's wrong."
2. "Yes, there seem to be many things that doctors don't know enough about." *or*
   "Oh, I believe you, and of course you must be very disappointed." *or*
   Isn't it a shame that there are so many problems that medicine hasn't solved yet." (with the intonation of a statement, not a question!) *or*
   "Oh, I know. It is upsetting."
3. "But do forgive me . . ."
4. "I'm very busy and have to finish writing this report immediately."

Demonstrate how you would politely interrupt the speaker in the following situations.
1. Your friend spends three or four minutes boring you with the plot of a movie. Then he or she says, "You know, it was one of the most entertaining films I've seen in a long time. It's much better than *Kiss Me, My Fool*. Now, in *that* movie . . . " Politely interrupt.
2. You meet a friend in a supermarket. He or she complains about the high cost of food and for several minutes compares the cost of various things today with their cost last year. And then you hear "Everything's getting so expensive that . . ." Politely interrupt.
3. A door-to-door salesman rings your doorbell and then explains nonstop why you should buy a new, improved laundry soap "because it cleans better and faster than any other soap on the market." Politely interrupt.

★★ With a partner, role-play one of the following situations in which one politely interrupts the other and ends the conversation. A should prepare a monologue of a minute or so. Once B interrupts, A should politely stop.

1. A is talking about the difficulties of his or her first day in English class.
2. A is explaining why he or she especially enjoys a television program.
3. A is describing a popular tourist attraction in his or her country.
4. A is telling about a misunderstanding that occurred between himself and his girlfriend/wife/boss or between herself and her boyfriend/husband/boss.
5. A is trying to sell an expensive, hard-cover, thumb-indexed English dictionary.

WRITING

Write a letter to Julie, as if you were Ann Landers, and answer her question.

VOCABULARY
insane
to commit a crime
train of thought
to clip
to hang on to
    something

from the desk of **ANN LANDERS**

Dear Julie,
The woman is hopelessly insane and unquestionably dangerous. She should be removed from society at once, before she commits some terrible crime, like interrupting your train of thought.

Kids like you make me sick. I'd give anything if my mother were around to "annoy" me like that. Clip this column and hang on to it. One day you'll see what I mean.

DISCUSSION

1. At what point in the letter do you realize that Ann Landers is being sarcastic?
2. Do you agree that Julie will someday see what Ann Landers means?
3. If you were Julie, how would you feel about Ann Landers' reply?

13

Hurt by Overheard Word

Dear Ann Landers,

I'm a 17-year-old guy who needs to know what to do. Right now I'm hurt, mad, insulted, and mixed up. This is the story.

I just phoned a girl I like a lot. We've dated some—not much, but I thought she liked me. When I asked her if I could come over after supper, she said, "Wait a minute." She thought she had the mouthpiece of the phone covered but I heard her say, "How can I get rid of this creep? He wants to come over and I don't want him to." Then she came back on and said, "I'm sorry but I have to go someplace with my parents."

I can't avoid this chick because we are in several classes together and we have the same friends. How should I act? Should I let her know that I heard what she said?

Double Ears

VOCABULARY

to overhear
a guy
mixed up
to date
to come over
to get rid of
a creep
to come back on
to avoid
a chick
Double Ears

FACTUAL QUESTIONS

1. Why did the boy telephone the girl? What did he ask her?
2. What did the girl say to him?
3. What did he accidentally overhear her say?
4. Why is he "hurt, mad, insulted, and mixed up?"
5. What questions does he ask Ann Landers?

LANGUAGE USE

The girl does not want the boy to visit her, but she doesn't want to be impolite and say this directly. She makes up a "white lie." This is a kind of lie that is considered harmless because it is told for the sake of being polite. What is a white lie called in your language? Is it considered socially acceptable?

DISCUSSION

1. If you were the boy, how would you feel?
2. If you were the girl, what would you do?
3. Has this kind of situation ever happened to you? What did you do?
4. Why didn't the girl make up an excuse immediately? Why do you suppose she needed to ask for help?
5. What do you think she might have said if the boy had asked if he could visit her the next night, or if he had asked for a date on the weekend?
6. What do you think Ann Landers will tell Double Ears to do?

LANGUAGE IN LIFE

★ Here are some white lies that might be said by someone who does not want to accept an invitation, but also does not want to admit it.

"Thanks a lot, but I have to do my homework."
"I'm sorry I can't come. I have a terrible headache."
"It's very thoughtful of you to ask. However, the baby is sick and we don't want to leave her with a babysitter."
"Thank you for inviting me, but I'll be out of town on that date."

Notice that each white lie has two parts: (1) *an expression of appreciation* of some kind, followed by (2) a contrived *explanation* of why the invitation cannot be accepted.

Prepare to respond to each of the following invitations by making up a reasonable white lie. Sound sincere.
1. "Would you like me to drive you home after class?"
2. "I didn't get to the bank today. I wonder if you could loan me $10 until tomorrow."
3. "Would you let me copy your composition? I didn't have time to do mine and yours are always so good."
4. "Can I borrow your car for an hour? I'm a very good driver."
5. "I'm trying a new recipe for breaded brains tonight. Why not come over and experience a new taste treat?"

Now work in pairs. Student A asks Student B to do something. Student B does not want to do it and makes up a white lie.

★★ With a partner, prepare to role-play the following conversation:

Boy	*Girl*
1. Telephone Maria.	1. Answer telephone.
2. Identify yourself and greet the girl politely.	2. Respond politely.
3. Ask if you can come over to visit her after supper. *(Show surprise and anger on your face.)*	3. Politely explain that you have to ask your parents. *(Cover mouthpiece of phone)* To someone in the room, explain that you don't want the boy to come over because "he's a creep." *(Speak on phone again)* Apologize. Explain the reason he can't come over.
4. Control your anger and express regret. Express hope you can visit some other time.	4. Express similar hope. Sound sincere. Politely say good bye.
5. Say good-bye.	5. *(Hang up)* Express annoyance with "the creep!"
6. *(Hang up)* Express annoyance.	

WRITING

Write a letter to Double Ears, as if you were Ann Landers, and answer his questions.

from the desk of **ANN LANDERS**

Dear Double Ears,
   Act natural. Don't let on that you heard her. Now that you know how she really feels, keep your distance and turn your attention elsewhere.

DISCUSSION
1. Do you agree with Ann Landers' advice?
2. Ann Landers advises Double Ears to "act natural." What does she mean? How should he act the next time he sees the girl?

14

Saddened by Separation

Dear Ann Landers,

I'm an 18-year-old girl, a freshman at the state university, and so lonesome for my guy I could just die.

Lou and I went steady the last two years of high school. We were really in love. (Anyone who says teenagers are too young to know what love is doesn't know what they are talking about.) We went everywhere and did everything together. Lou was the most important thing in my life. He felt the same about me.

Our folks decided it would be best if we went to different colleges. They said we should date others, that we weren't being fair to ourselves. We had to do it their way or forget about college and go to work. So off we went in different directions, agreeing to write letters, speak on the phone once a week (for five minutes) and date others.

It's been just hell. I'm sorry I agreed to this dumb arrangement. I live for Lou's letters and our weekly phone call. I cry every night. He has taken out a couple of girls and says they were "O.K., but nothing special." I haven't seen one dude here who can shine Lou's shoes.

I think our parents were cruel to do this to us. We were *so* happy, and now we are both miserable. Say something, please.

In Dante's Inferno

VOCABULARY
to go steady
to date
had to do it their way
hell
dumb
a dude
Dante's Inferno

FACTUAL QUESTIONS
1. How long did Lou and the girl go steady?
2. How did she and Lou feel about each other?
3. Why did their parents think that they should go to different colleges?
4. What did Lou and the girl agree to do?
5. Why did they agree to do it?
6. What has life been like for the girl?
7. How often does Lou call?
8. What does she want Ann Landers to do?

LANGUAGE USE

Notice the use of the singular and plural forms: "*Anyone* who *says* . . . *doesn't* know what *they are* talking about." *Anyone, anybody, everyone, everybody* are followed by a singular verb. In informal English, a plural pronoun is often used to avoid saying *he* or *she,* since there is no single word for this. Example: *Everyone must leave their hats and coats* instead of *Everyone must leave his or her hat and coat. Everybody's here now, aren't they?* instead of . . . *isn't he or she?* Have you heard people say this? What other ungrammatical forms do you hear people use in informal situations?

DISCUSSION

1. Do you agree that "anyone who says teenagers are too young to know what love is doesn't know what they are talking about"?
2. Were the parents cruel to separate their children? What might have been their reason for doing this?
3. Is it fair, or wise, for parents to use threats? For example: Do it our way or forget about college.
4. What does the writer mean when she says, "I haven't seen one dude here who can shine Lou's shoes?" How else could she express this feeling?
5. What do you think the girl wants Ann Landers to say?

WRITING

Write a letter, as if you were Ann Landers, in which you "Say something" to this girl.

Dear Dante,

You *will* live through the year and be better for it. In the meantime, date others and make an effort to get involved in campus activities.

Your parents did you both a favor. You'll appreciate their wisdom when the year is over and you and Lou have proved—not only to them, but to yourselves—that what you have is the real thing.

DISCUSSION

1. In what way(s) do you think they will be better for having been separated for a year?
2. Why do you think Ann Landers agrees with the parents and says that their children should date others during the year?
3. What is "the real thing"?

LANGUAGE IN LIFE

★ Assume the year has passed. The girls that Lou dated became something more than "nothing special" and Lou and the letter-writer have now broken up. The girl is angry with her parents. Being angry often includes directly blaming someone. For example:

You're to blame for this!

It's all your fault!

This wouldn't have happened if you hadn't forced us to separate!

Notice the various patterns for *if*-clauses:

He		left me		you hadn't made us date others.
You	wouldn't have	wrecked my car	if	you had been driving more carefully.
My bicycle		been stolen		you had locked it properly.

Assume that you are very angry because of the following situations. Choose someone in class and blame him or her. Make up a reasonable *if*-clause.

1. Your car, which you loaned to someone, was stolen.
2. Someone dropped and broke your expensive calculator.
3. At a pizza parlor, someone bumped into you and spilled pizza all over your sweater.
4. Someone borrowed your camera and lost it.
5. Someone told a lie about you to a close friend and now your friend won't speak to you.

★★ Assume that Lou's girlfriend (give her a name) and her mother or father are talking at the end of the year. The daughter blames her parents for the breakup of their "real love." The parent denies responsibility.

Daughter	*Parent*
1. Express unhappiness. Blame your parents for forcing such "a dumb arrangement" on you and Lou.	1. Express sympathy for your daughter's unhappiness, but deny responsibility.
2. Explain that your love was real and would have survived if Lou had not been forced to date other girls.	2. Explain that if the love had been real it would have survived the year apart.
3. Express anger. Once again blame your parents for being cruel and for making you so miserable.	3. Express unhappiness that your daughter blames you. Assure her that she will appreciate your wisdom some day.

15

Dare to Discipline?

Dear Ann Landers,
My husband and I have been firm with our own children. They are well-behaved, considerate youngsters, 5 and 7. But we are having serious difficulty with the children of some close friends that is threatening our relationship with them. Please help.

Our two must be in bed at 8:00 PM on weekdays and 9:00 PM on non-school nights. Frequently these friends bring their two to sleep at our home. They are permitted to watch TV and roam about the house as late as 2:00 AM! Apparently they are also permitted to help themselves to whatever is in the refrigerator at home, so they do the same thing at our home. These youngsters eat all evening long.

My husband and I like this couple very much but their kids are a pain in the neck. Do we have the right to discipline them when they are in our home and their parents are present but unconcerned?

Annoyed

FACTUAL QUESTIONS
1. How old are the writer's children? At what time do they go to bed?
2. How do their friends' children behave? What do they do?
3. Does the writer like the friends? The friends' children?
4. What question does she ask?

DISCUSSION

VOCABULARY
firm
considerate
youngsters
to threaten
to roam
apparently
to discipline
to be annoyed
a pain in the neck

1. These young children are required to go to bed at 8:00 on school nights and 9:00 on non-school nights. Did you have a strict bedtime as a child? Did you have a curfew as a teenager? (A *curfew* is a set time by which you have to be home.)
2. Do you feel it is desirable to raise children with much stricter discipline than your neighbors' or friends' children?
3. If Annoyed and her husband are worried about their friendship with the couple, why don't they talk it over with them directly? Why might they want Ann Landers' opinion before they discuss it with the couple?

LANGUAGE IN LIFE
Review expressions of displeasure and prohibition in Letter Number 10.

★ Expressions of displeasure are often followed by a request or demand to change behavior. For example:

You must You have to	stop	making so much noise. roaming about the house. watching television. your child from eating so much.
Would you please		go to bed now. be quiet! say goodnight to everyone and go upstairs to bed.

Express displeasure by giving an order, either to stop doing something or to do something different.

1. Your classmate regularly makes jokes about your country.
2. Someone's cat is digging up your flower garden.
3. Your friend drives too fast.
4. Someone's handwriting is almost impossible to read.
5. Your friend has been talking on the telephone for more than an hour.
6. Your neighbor's dog has been barking for an hour.
7. Someone's radio is very loud.
8. Someone continually blows smoke in your face.
9. Your friend is drinking too much at a party.
10. Your friend keeps interrupting while you're trying to tell a joke.

WRITING
Write a letter to Annoyed, as if you were Ann Landers, and answer her question.

from the desk of **ANN LANDERS**

Dear Annoyed,
   Yes, you do and I hope you will. And
don't be surprised if the kids like it.
Children don't really enjoy running wild
and doing as they please. They like to be
told who's who and what's what. It gives
them the idea that they are worth
bothering about and that someone cares
about them.

LANGUAGE USE

Ann Landers answers, "Yes, you do and I hope you will." We often use short forms to
respond to questions. What are the questions she is answering? What is the full answer:
do what? *will* what?

DISCUSSION

1. Do you agree that children want to be disciplined, or is this the wishful thought of
   grown-ups?
2. In what ways might Annoyed discipline her own children? Her friends' children?
3. If being told who's who and what's what gives children the idea that they are worth
   bothering about, wouldn't it be better that parents do this? Why do you suppose Ann
   Landers has not urged Annoyed to first speak to the parents?

LANGUAGE IN LIFE

★ If Annoyed expresses displeasure to the children, she might include a direct order, such as the following:

Don't turn on the television.
You mustn't make so much noise.
You have to go to bed now.
Please stop opening the refrigerator.

If she expresses her displeasure to the parents instead of the children, she would use one of the following indirect forms:

Please tell your child not to turn on the television.
Would you tell her to stop running about the house.
Please ask him not to open the refrigerator any more.

Notice the various patterns of an indirect order:

| (Please) tell | someone your children your friend | (not) | to turn on the TV. to drive fast. |
| | | to stop | making so much noise. driving so fast. |

Make indirect orders for the ten situations on page 64.

16

Invitation is Incomplete

Dear Ann Landers,
Four years ago, at the age of 17, I told my parents I was going to become engaged to a man they despised. They tried to talk me out of it but my mind was made up. I should tell you that Robert was six years my senior and handicapped. They informed me that if I accepted a ring from him, I must move out of the house at once. So I did, and moved in with Robert.

Eleven months later our child was born. We decided to get married three weeks after that by the Justice of the Peace. I phoned my mother, with whom I had had little contact those several months, and told her about the baby. She said she had heard the news and she and my father would like to see me but Robert was not welcome in their home. He is very hurt but feels I should take the baby and go see them.

I don't know what to do, Ann. I know my folks are dying to see their first grandchild, but I hate to hurt my husband. Please advise.

Asunder in Ohio

VOCABULARY
to despise
to become engaged
talk me out of it
my mind was made up
Robert was six years
    my senior
if I accepted a ring
    from him
contact
dying to see their first
    grandchild
asunder

FACTUAL QUESTIONS
1. Why did the writer of this letter move out of her parents' house? Where did she move?
2. When did she telephone her mother? Why?
3. What did her mother tell her?
4. What does her husband think she should do?
5. What specific advice does she want?

DISCUSSION

1. What is the decision she has to make?
2. The writer says that her parents despised Robert but doesn't explain why. What reasons might they have?
3. Were the parents wise to threaten their daughter?
4. Was the daughter right to marry against her parents' wishes?
5. If someone is going to be hurt, is it better to be this woman's husband or parents?
6. If the daughter hadn't written for Ann Landers' advice, what do you think she would have done on her own?

LANGUAGE IN LIFE

Robert advises his wife to take the baby and go see her parents. Affirmative and negative advice can be expressed in the following ways:

It would (not) be			a good idea (un)wise/(im)polite (un)helpful/(un)thoughtful	(not) to go.
I	(don't)	advise urge	you	
		think that		should (not) go. ought (not) to go.

★ Choose someone in class and give him or her some affirmative or negative advice. Use your own or some of the following ideas.

1. Study your English.
2. Buy a new car now.
3. Stop smoking.
4. Learn the irregular verbs.
5. Be more careful while driving.
6. Eat less junk food.
7. Write a letter home.
8. Spend $80 for a guitar.
9. Get more sleep.
10. Use so many swearwords in public.

WRITING

Write a letter to Asunder in Ohio, as if you were Ann Landers, and advise her what to do.

VOCABULARY

to relent
to reject
a closed door
to risk
build bridges—not
    fences

from the desk of **ANN LANDERS**

Dear Asunder,
    Take the baby and go see them. In time perhaps they will relent and accept Robert. If you reject this invitation, it might mean a closed door for all time. Don't risk it. Now is the time to build bridges—not fences.

DISCUSSION

1. Do you think Robert will be hurt by the advice that Ann Landers gives?
2. Give examples of other situations when it might be better to build bridges, not fences.

LANGUAGE IN LIFE

★★ During the conversation on the telephone between the daughter and her mother, the daughter didn't know what to say. She had to delay a decision. She might have expressed her uncertainty by any of the following:

I need time to check with Robert. May I let you know later?
Let me discuss it with Robert and answer you later.
I would like to think about it and call you back later.
I'd like to think about it. Can I call you back later?

When someone in your class speaks to you, politely express uncertainty and delay a decision. For example:

Invite B to dinner on Saturday night.
A: I'm having a small dinner party on Saturday night. I would like to have you come.
B: Thank you very much. But I have to check with my wife. May I let you know tomorrow?

1. Ask C to study English with you tonight.
2. Suggest to D that you go to the movies together tonight.
3. Ask E if you can borrow his or her car this weekend.
4. Invite F to accompany you to the annual meeting of the Miniature Tree-Growers Association.
5. Request G to take care of your three cats for the weekend.
6. Invite H to an all-day family reunion.
7. Tell J that you need $100 immediately. Ask if he or she will lend it to you.
8. Suggest to K that you both invite your teacher to dinner.

17

Beard Bothers Bride

Dear Ann Landers,
Six months ago our son Jack announced his plans to be married. At that time he asked his younger brother Don to be his best man. Don said he would. Since that time Don has grown a full beard and mustache and his hair is quite a bit longer. I am the mother and while I am not crazy about the way the boy looks, he does keep himself clean and neat. Incidentally, Jack is 23 and Don is 19.

Last night Jack's fiancée was here for dinner. She said she would not allow Don to be in the wedding party unless he cut off the beard and shortened his hair. Don said he had no intention of doing either and that unless he was acceptable as he is, he would not attend the wedding even as a guest.

This has created a serious problem in our family and we don't know what to say or do. Will you please give us the benefit of your wisdom and experience?

Evanston, Illinois

FACTUAL QUESTIONS
1. What did Jack ask his brother to do?
2. What has Don done since then?
3. How does Jack's fiancée feel about it?
4. What does she tell Don?
5. What is Don's answer?
6. What does the mother want from Ann Landers?

VOCABULARY
best man
to be crazy about
incidentally
fiancée
an intention
benefit
wisdom

LANGUAGE USE
Fiancée is a word borrowed from the French language. What other words are used in English that come from other languages? What English words have become part of *your* language?

DISCUSSION

1. How does his mother feel about Don's appearance?
2. Why do you suppose Don's appearance so upsets Jack's fiancée?
3. Is it fair to Don or Jack for the fiancée to set this condition?
4. Which side do you suppose Jack is on?
5. Do you sympathize most with Don, Jack, Jack's fiancée, or the mother? Why?

LANGUAGE IN LIFE

★ Assume that Jack's fiancée and Don are talking about the wedding. She tells Don that she does not like his long hair and beard. Then she states a condition:

Fiancée: You can be in the wedding if you shave off your beard.
Don: But I don't want to. I refuse to shave it off.
Fiancée: Well then, if you won't shave off your beard, you can't be in the wedding.

Practice a short dialogue in which (1) you state an affirmative condition, (2) your partner refuses or makes a negative statement, so (3) you express a negative condition with a negative result. For example:

A: You'll like that book if you enjoy science-fiction.
B: But I don't enjoy science-fiction.
A: Well, if you don't enjoy science-fiction, then you won't like that book.

1. You can learn English if you study harder.
2. You'll feel better in the morning if you go to bed earlier at night.
3. You can pass the test if you study all the irregular verbs.
4. You can live a long, healthy life if you stop smoking.
5. You'll like this pizza if you like pepperoni.
6. You could be a great tennis player if you practiced at least four hours a day.
7. You're allowed to eat in that restaurant only if you're willing to put on a coat and tie.
8. You'll enjoy the movie *Jaws II* if you enjoyed *Jaws I*.

★★ Notice how *wishes* can be expressed:

I wish (that)	you hadn't grown a beard.
	you didn't have such long hair.
	you weren't so mean to your sister.
	you would cut off your beard.
	your hair weren't so long.
	your hair were shorter.

Prepare the following role-play between Jack's fiancée (give her a name) and Don.

Fiancée	*Don*
1. Politely state that you do not like Don's beard and long hair. Express wish that he shave off his beard and cut his hair for the wedding.	1. Politely accept her statement. Ask why she doesn't like your beard and long hair.
2. Explain that all the men in the wedding party will be neat and clean-shaven.	2. Reply that your hair and beard are neat, and that you have no intention of shaving your beard or cutting your hair.
3. Try to persuade Don to shave. Explain importance of wedding to you and Jack and that everything must look right.	3. State that you would not look right without your long hair and beard.
4. Emphatically state your condition: he cannot be in the wedding if he does not shave off his beard and cut his hair.	4. Reply appropriately.

WRITING

Write a letter to the mother, as if you were Ann Landers, and give her "the benefit of your wisdom and experience."

from the desk of ANN LANDERS

Dear Evanston,
   The choice of the best man is one of the few privileges of the groom. If he selects King Kong, the bride should go along with his choice. I hope your future daughter-in-law changes her mind. If Don does not attend the wedding, she will have created a rift between brothers that could last a lifetime. This is no way to start a marriage.

CULTURAL NOTE

In the United States the bride's family traditionally plans and pays for a formal wedding and reception. The groom and his family may be consulted but, except for his choice of best man and ushers, the groom contributes little more than the ring. What are the marriage customs in your country? Who organizes the wedding and decides on matters such as this?

DISCUSSION

1. How do you think Jack's fiancée will accept Ann Landers' advice?
2. If she doesn't accept the advice, what do you think Jack should do?

18

Calling Collect; Lack of Respect?

Dear Ann Landers,
My boyfriend, who is 19 years old, moved to another city. I am 17, work part-time and do baby-sitting, so I have money of my own. (I get no allowance.)

Lately I've been having terrific hassles with my parents. When Jed calls me collect, they refuse to accept the call, even though I am sitting right there. They just say, "Marianne isn't at home." I don't mind paying for his calls, and as long as it's my money I don't think they have the right to do this.

My mother says in her day no respectable boy called a girl collect, and no decent girl would accept such a call. Jed has a job but he's just getting by and the only way we can talk is if I pay on my end.

We'd like your opinion on this.

The Sound of His Voice

FACTUAL QUESTIONS
1. What is the hassle that this girl has with her parents?
2. Why doesn't Jed pay for his telephone calls?
3. How is his girl friend able to pay for them?
4. Why does the mother refuse to accept collect calls from Jed?

VOCABULARY
an allowance
a hassle
to call collect
to refuse
to accept
(not) to mind doing
    something
in her day
respectable
decent
to just get by

CULTURAL NOTES
1. A telephone book defines a collect call by explaining: "You may place calls and charge them to the number you are calling, provided the person you are calling agrees to accept the charges." Explain in your own words.
2. Older people often express unhappiness with the current state of the world by comparing the present with the past. They say, "In my day . . ." How do you feel when you hear this? Have you ever used this expression?

DISCUSSION

1. Do you think it is proper for a boy to call his girl friend collect? Would it be proper for her to call him collect?
2. If a teenager earns money, should he or she have the right to decide how to spend it?
3. Could the girl send her boyfriend money so he wouldn't have to call collect? Do you think he would be willing to accept cash as easily as he does free phone calls?
4. What do you think the girl wants Ann Landers to tell her?

LANGUAGE IN LIFE

★ To make a collect telephone call, you must speak to the operator. The following dialogue might occur:

You: I'd like to make a collect call, please. The area code is 905. The number is 244-7358. My name is _____ .

Operator: Thank you. Just a minute please.
          (*The telephone is answered.*) I have a collect call from _____ .
          Will you accept the charges?

Notice the customary way that telephone numbers are spoken:
1. Zero is pronounced as if it were the letter O: *oh*. 905 = nine-oh-five.
2. Numbers are spoken separately. 244 = two-four-four, not *two hundred forty-four*, or *two-double-four*.
3. There is a slight pause between the exchange number (244) and the individual number (7358): two-four-four (*pause*) seven-three-five-eight.

With a partner, practice making collect telephone calls. Use these numbers:
    (212) 748-2810   (415) 922-1833
    (809) 132-0704   (416) 553-6768
    (202) 485-4938   (212) 736-5000

★★ Disapproval can be expressed in a number of ways. In this case, the mother might have told her daughter:
    "I don't approve of his calling you collect."

Or she may give the reason for her disapproval:
    "It's not proper for a decent girl to accept collect calls from boys."

Prepare to role-play the following conversations. In the first, the mother explains her disapproval to Marianne. In the second, Jed's father explains his disapproval to his son.

Mother	*Marianne*
1. Express disapproval of Jed's calling collect.	1. Explain it is your money and you can use it for any purpose you want.
2. Agree. Explain, however, that this is a wrong use of her money. It is not proper.	2. Express surprise. Ask why it is not proper.
3. Answer (by reference to lines 16–18).	3. Express disagreement. Explain that "times have changed."
4. Insist that respectability and decency never change. Repeat your disapproval.	4. Explain that *you* will then telephone *him!*

Father	*Jed*
1. Express disapproval of your son's calling Marianne collect.	1. Explain you don't have the money. Marianne does, and she doesn't mind paying for the calls.
2. Explain that it is not gentlemanly or proper.	2. Express surprise. Ask what is ungentlemanly or improper about it.
3. Answer (by reference to lines 16–18).	3. Express disagreement. Explain that "times have changed."
4. Insist that respectability and decency never change. Repeat disapproval.	4. Reluctantly accept his disapproval. Then ask *him* to pay for your calls to Marianne.

WRITING

Write a letter to The Sound of His Voice, as if you were Ann Landers, and give your opinion about this hassle.

VOCABULARY
a principle
you have a point
practically
an emergency
to demonstrate
a lack of
   integrity
a surplus

from the desk of **ANN LANDERS**

Dear Voice,

In principle you have a point. It's your money and if you want to spend it on collect calls from Jed, you should be able to do it.

Practically, however, your mother is right. A fellow who would call his girl collect, except in case of emergency, demonstrates a lack of integrity and a surplus of poor judgment.

DISCUSSION

1. In effect, Ann Landers says "In principle you're right, in practice you're wrong." Do you think this response will satisfy the girl? Her parents?
2. Do you agree that a man demonstrates a lack of integrity if he telephones his girl friend collect? Is Ann Landers sexist and old-fashioned?
3. In what situations (from whom) would you accept a collect call?

19

Should She or Shouldn't She?

Dear Ann Landers,

My parents and I have been carrying on a running argument for three months. Will you please try to see all sides of the question and answer it honestly?

My boyfriend and I have been going together for over a year. We plan to get married when he finds a job he really likes. I am working but I live at home and have to pay room and board.

I want to move out of my parents' house and live with my fiancé. We could make it financially with my check added to his. My folks are against it. They say it is immoral. We say it's sensible. We just might find out after we live together awhile that we don't like each other well enough to spend the rest of our lives together.

Isn't it better to shack up for a time than to get married, find out you've made a mistake and then get a divorce? How else can two people really learn *all* about one another's little quirks? What do you say?

M. and B.

VOCABULARY
a running argument
to see all sides of the
    question
room and board
fiancé
to make it
(im)moral
sensible
to shack up
a divorce
a quirk

FACTUAL QUESTIONS
1. How long have the writer and her parents been arguing?
2. What is the first question she asks Ann Landers?
3. How long have M and B been going together?
4. When do they plan to marry?
5. Where is the girl living now?
6. What does she want to do? Why?
7. What do her parents think of the idea?
8. What questions does the girl ask?

CULTURAL NOTES

1. A change in moral attitudes has occurred in the United States during the last 25 or 30 years. In the past very few couples considered it respectable to live together before marriage. Accurate statistics are difficult to obtain, but the idea has now become common enough so that most people are no longer shocked, although they may still disagree about its appropriateness. Do you think the attitudes of M and B (the younger generation) and the parents (the older generation) are characteristic of the American population as a whole?

2. This girl is working but she is living at home. Her parents have asked her to contribute to the household expenses. Do you think this is often done in American families? What reasons might there be for such an arrangement?

DISCUSSION

1. In your country, if you were working but living at home, would you be expected to pay for your room and board?

2. Is it possible for a young unmarried couple in your country to live together? Is there a difference in attitude between the younger and the older generations?

3. The writer of this letter argues that living together before marriage is sensible. Her parents argue that it is immoral. Why are they not likely to come to an agreement?

LANGUAGE IN LIFE

★ If you believe that something is (or is not) true, you can use any of the following patterns:

I	am	certain sure convinced	(that) . . .
	think believe		

For example:

DAUGHTER: I believe that it is sensible for a couple to live together before marriage.

MOTHER: I'm convinced that it's immoral.

DAUGHTER: I don't think you understand my viewpoint.

MOTHER: I'm sure I do, and I'm certain that I don't agree with it.

Practice stating your beliefs about some of the following topics:
1. Classes in the early morning/late afternoon/in the evening.
2. English spelling/pronunciation/idioms.
3. Your favorite car/singer/movie/food.
4. The cost of living/clothes/books/gasoline/food.
5. American food/clothes/customs/television/geography.
6. Life in a big city/small town/in a dormitory/on campus.

To be persuasive, a statement of belief is often followed by a *because*-clause that states a reason. For example:

DAUGHTER: I believe it's sensible for us to live together because we'll be able to find out if we like each other well enough to spend the rest of our lives together.
MOTHER: No, I think you're mistaken. I believe it's immoral because you must be married, at least legally if not actually in a church, before you live together.

Practice stating your belief about some of the topics above, this time stating at least one reason. For example:
I think English spelling is difficult because so many words are not spelled the way they are pronounced.

★★ Students who are strongly and seriously committed to one side of a topic or the other should prepare to argue their position. The reasons are usually stated in order of importance; in other words, the most persuasive is given first. Sometimes, however, for dramatic effect the best or most important reason is held until the end, where it is emphatic like a knockout punch.

WRITING
Write a reply, as if you were Ann Landers, in which you answer the girl's question: "What do you say?"

from the desk of **ANN LANDERS**

Dear M. and B.,

Sorry, but shacking up isn't the same thing as being married. Moreover, the evidence is on the other side. A recent survey showed that couples who lived together before marriage had a higher divorce rate than those who didn't play house before the ceremony. And what's more, the divorces tended to be filed within the first two years of these marriages.

DISCUSSION

1. Ann Landers refers directly to the parents' moral argument by making an undefined distinction between "shacking up" and "being married." Her main argument, however, is based on statistical information which challenges the "sensible" viewpoint of the girl. Do you think this is the answer she expected or hoped for? Has Ann Landers tried "to see all sides of this question and answer it honestly"?
2. What attitudes does Ann Landers reveal by using an image of childhood behavior: "play house before the ceremony"?

LANGUAGE IN LIFE

★ With a partner, role-play the following conversation between the girl and one of her parents. Assume that the parent is sympathetic and genuinely responds to the daughter's feelings, but is unable to agree.

Daughter	*Parent*
1. Explain your desire to move out of the house and move in with (give your boyfriend a name).	1. Express understanding of your daughter's feelings, but express belief that it would be immoral.
2. Express belief that your parents' morality is out of date. Express belief that it is sensible to live together before getting married.	2. Express agreement that it might *seem* sensible, but quote the statistical information in Ann Landers' reply.

★★ With a partner, role-play the following conversation between the girl and one of her parents. Assume that the parent is strict and dictatorial.

Daughter	*Parent*
1. Explain your desire to move out of the house and move in with (give your boyfriend a name).	1. Express surprise and displeasure. Express belief that it would be morally wrong.
2. Express belief that your parents' morality is out of date. Express belief that it would be sensible to live together before getting married. Give at least two reasons.	2. Criticize your daughter for questioning your judgment. Criticize her reasoning. Quote the statistical information in Ann Landers' reply (but do not give source).
3. Express disagreement with the statistics and state that you will write Ann Landers.	3. State the source of the statistics. Express belief in their accuracy.

20

Parents' Patience Wearing Thin

Dear Ann Landers,
Our darling daughter married at 18 right after high school graduation. We tried our best to get her to go to college or work for a year, but her mind was made up.

The boy she married is 19. My husband and I disliked him from the start. He was sloppy, ill-mannered, and lazy. Our daughter saw none of these qualities and would not listen to a word of criticism.

Now, after a year (and a baby), he has no job and the three of them are living with us. Both my husband and I work, and our son-in-law stays home, collects unemployment compensation, and watches TV. My husband's patience is wearing thin and so is mine. Whenever I start to say something, my daughter cries and begs me to leave him alone and give him a chance.

We can't throw him out on the street, Ann. What can we do?

Trapped

VOCABULARY
a graduation
to make up one's mind
sloppy
ill-mannered
lazy
criticism
compensation
patience is wearing
  thin
to beg
to leave someone
  alone
trapped

FACTUAL QUESTIONS
1. Who wrote this letter?
2. Why don't the parents like their daughter's husband?
3. What happened to the young couple after a year of marriage?
4. While both parents work, what does her husband do?

CULTURAL NOTE
What is unemployment compensation? What is it intended for? Have you or anyone you know ever received unemployment compensation?

LANGUAGE USE

What does the use of "Our darling daughter" at the very beginning tell you about the mother's attitude toward the girl? What does it tell you about her probable attitude toward the girl's husband?

DISCUSSION

1. Why do you think the daughter didn't want to go to college or work?
2. Why does the writer feel trapped?
3. The mother claims, "We can't throw them out in the street." Do you agree? Is there some other alternative?
4. The problem in Letter Number 16 is somewhat the same. What might have happened if these parents had handled it in the same way as the parents of Asunder in Ohio?
5. What do you feel is the responsibility of parents to their children, once they leave home, work, or get married?
6. Do you think the daughter and/or her husband are really unwelcome? Would they be welcome under different circumstances?

LANGUAGE IN LIFE

★ *To plead* is to make continual, emotional requests. For example, the daughter might have pleaded:

Please don't shout at him.
I beg you to give him a chance.

Notice the various ways in which *a plea* can be expressed:

Please (don't)			leave him alone. give him a chance.
I'm	asking begging	you (not) to	blame him. condemn him.

Plead with someone who regularly:

1. steps on your flower garden.
2. eats garlic in bed.
3. tells your friends how cute you were as a baby.
4. forgets to return your borrowed dictionary.
5. gets drunk and insults people.
6. embarrasses you by telling dirty jokes.

★★ Assume that the father's patience finally wears too thin. He becomes very angry. He expresses his anger by shouting:

$$\text{I'm} \quad \begin{array}{|c|} \text{angry} \\ \text{mad} \end{array} \quad \text{as hell!}$$

You may also hear less emphatic expressions of anger, such as:
    I'm as angry as can be!
    She was (as) angry as could be!
    He was madder than a hornet!
    She's as mad as a wet hen!

If he orders his son-in-law to get out and find a job, he might shout angrily:

$$\text{You've got to} \quad \begin{array}{|l} \text{get out!} \\ \text{leave!} \\ \text{get out of here!} \\ \text{find a job!} \\ \text{stop lying around doing nothing!} \end{array}$$

For each of the following situations, express your anger by shouting an order.
1. Someone regularly steps on your flower garden.
2. Your neighbor's three cats howl all night.
3. Your roommate leaves dirty clothes and used towels lying all about the room.
4. Your friend has just been given his or her seventh speeding ticket in seven days.
5. Your roommate carelessly leaves lighted cigarettes around, burning holes in the carpet, table tops, and bed spreads.

WRITING
Write a letter to Trapped, as if you were Ann Landers, and suggest what they can do.

from the desk of ANN LANDERS

VOCABULARY

board
to sponge
parasitic
  (a parasite)
hospitality
to cripple

Dear Trapped,

So long as you provide bed and board (and TV), you are going to have these "house guests" with you. And why not? It's easier to sponge than to go to work.

Tell your daughter and son-in-law that they have 30 days to find a place of their own—which means he'll have to go to work. You are doing them no favor in allowing them to continue this parasitic existence. In fact, your hospitality is crippling the boy emotionally.

DISCUSSION

1. Do you think Ann Landers is right to call the daughter and son-in-law "house guests"? Is she fair to refer to their need to live with their in-laws as *sponging* or a *parasitic existence?*
2. Are the parents likely to take this advice? Could the couple find a job and a place to live in thirty days?

21

In-Laws Demand Helping Hand

Dear Ann Landers,
Most of the letters that appear in your column come from city people. Please print a problem that might be boring to your urban readers, but farm folks need help too.

My husband and I have been married fifteen years. We have five children and we get along fine. The only thorn in my side is my in-laws. They have the farm next to ours and we end up doing all their hard work.

Every morning for fifteen years my father-in-law has telephoned my husband before breakfast, or worse, has come over here in person and told my husband what to do, as if he were a small child. If we are at the breakfast table, my father-in-law pulls up a chair and tells him to hurry up.

When my in-laws go on vacations, we are expected to do the chores. They cannot do our chores when we go on vacation because they can barely handle their own. So, when we leave town, we have to hire help. I feel they should do the same.

My husband has two brothers but they were a lot smarter than he was. They went to college and got away from their parents. It burns me up to listen to them and their wives tell us how comforting it is to know that the folks have somebody near to help them, now that they are getting on in years.

We can't move so please don't suggest it, Ann. Just tell me if there is any way to get a grown man to cut himself loose from his parents so he and his family can lead their own lives.

Dakota Plight

VOCABULARY
urban
a thorn in my side
to end up
to get burned up
to get on in years
a plight

FACTUAL QUESTIONS
1. Where does the writer of this letter live?
2. Are the writer and her husband happily married?
3. What is the thorn in her side?
4. What happens when her in-laws go on vacation?
5. What happens when her family goes on vacation?
6. Why does she resent her husband's brothers?
7. What question does the woman ask?
8. In what state does she live?

DISCUSSION
1. Why do you suppose the two farms are next to each other?
2. Do you think the two brothers are younger than the writer's husband? Would this explain why he must give more help to his parents than his brothers do?
3. Does the statement "they were a lot smarter . . . they went to college . . ." mean that her husband was less intelligent than his brothers and therefore was not admitted to a college?
4. How do you think the husband feels about the situation?
5. Do you think the husband would agree with the question which his wife asks at the end of her letter? Is there any indication in the letter that he is unhappy with the present arrangement?

LANGUAGE IN LIFE
★ The woman writes that the brothers and their wives "tell us how comforting it is to know that the folks have somebody near to help them . . ." They might have said:
   How comforting it is to know that you're so near!
In this expression, *how* is used, not to ask a question, but to introduce an exclamation. Note that *how* is followed by an adjective, and sometimes a clause:

	beautiful!
	easy it was!
How	kind of you to help!
	dirty this room is!
	happy I am to see you!

Make an exclamation, introduced by *how,* about each of the following ideas.
1. the beauty of the Taj Mahal
2. the difficulty of irregular verbs
3. the usefulness of computers
4. the greatness of a national hero
5. the speed of modern travel
6. the music of a famous rock group
7. the traffic in your capital city
8. the taste of liver and onions

★★ Make an exclamation, introduced by *how,* about each of the following situations. For example: You lock your keys in the car.
   How stupid of me!   *or*
   How careless!   *or*
   How silly of me to do this!

1. A friend brings you chicken soup when you are sick in bed.
2. You meet a good friend whom you've not seen in three years.

3. You tell someone about a party that was very boring.
4. Your friend helps you with your English homework.
5. The next-door neighbors were very noisy last night.
6. A stranger takes time to draw you a map of how to get to the bus station.
7. You apologize for not having written your family for a month.
8. You express your feelings about the sunrise.

★ The writer of this letter might ask her husband: "How come we always have to do your parents' chores when they go away but they never do ours?" *How come* is an informal way to ask a question that means "Why is it that . . . ?"

Ask a question about each of the following situations, using *How come . . . ?* First, ask the person. Then ask someone else about the person. For example:
A wasn't at the party last night.
"How come you weren't at the party last night?"
"*B,* how come *A* wasn't at the party last night?"

1. *B* always knows when it's going to rain.
2. *C* doesn't like your new wristwatch.
3. *D* has a new hair style.
4. *E* was absent yesterday.
5. *F* doesn't want to go home for Christmas.
6. *G* hasn't finished the homework yet.
7. *H* likes Mrs. Smith, but not Mr. Smith.
8. *J* was very unhappy last night.
9. *K* has never learned how to drive.
10. *L* is such a lazy student.

★★ *And how!* is an exclamation that informally expresses an emphatic "Yes!" It means "Very much so." For example:
"Did you have a good vacation?" "And how!"

To each of the following questions and statements, reply affirmatively with the exclamation "And how!"
1. Are you homesick?
2. It's a beautiful, beautiful day.
3. Were you a good student in your previous school?
4. That was a great party last night, wasn't it?
5. The food in the cafeteria is delicious/awful.
Continue, one student making a question or statement to which the next student can respond with "And how!"

WRITING

Write a letter to Dakota Plight, as if you were Ann Landers, and give your opinion about the situation.

VOCABULARY
insoluble
to be tied up
to compromise
hostility

from the desk of ANN LANDERS

Dear Dakota,
Your problem is as close to insoluble as any I've ever read. Not only is your husband tied up financially with his parents (I'll bet they gave him his farm), but worse, he is tied up emotionally in a way that his brothers are not—which is probably why they left and he stayed.

Ask your husband to compromise on one point. He should tell his parents that he can't handle their chores when they take vacations. Suggest that from now on they hire the same man *you* hire when you go away. If he agrees, it will reduce your hostility.

DISCUSSION

1. Can you think of any other suggestions?
2. How come Ann Landers realizes that it's impossible for the husband to break himself away from his parents but his wife doesn't?

91

LANGUAGE IN LIFE

★ Capability and incapability can be expressed by using any of the following: *can, able, possible*. For example:

I	am able to	do my chores, but	I	am	unable not able to	do yours.
	can				cannot	
It's possible for me to			it's impossible not possible to			

Practice expressing capability and incapability by telling what you can and cannot do. Use different forms from the table above. For example:

  I can ski pretty well but I'm not able to skate at all.

  It's impossible for me to meet you after class today, but I can meet you for coffee
    tomorrow morning.

22

Food for Sitter; Mother Bitter

Dear Ann Landers,
Occasionally my husband and I can squeeze an evening out on our budget. This includes a babysitter for two children. It seems lately that our babysitters are costing us double and triple, but not in wages. It's food. Both girls are related to us and I don't want to fire them because it would cause hard feelings in the family.

I always leave a snack for the sitter, but when I return I find she has devoured the tuna salad or luncheon meat I was saving for my husband's lunch. She opens cans of fruit, cuts into cakes and pies I prepare for the bridge club, and uses a quarter pound of butter to put over popcorn.

I have told both sitters what to eat and what *not* to eat, but it does no good. Now, what do I do, Ann Landers?

No Tightwad but No Rockefeller Either

VOCABULARY
to be bitter
to squeeze
an evening out
a budget
a babysitter
double
triple
wages
to fire someone
hard feelings
a snack
to devour
tuna salad
luncheon meat
a bridge club
a tightwad
Rockefeller

FACTUAL QUESTIONS
1. Is this couple very wealthy?
2. How many children do they have?
3. How many babysitters do they employ (at different times)?
4. Is the babysitter paid for looking after the children in the evening?
5. Why is it so expensive for this couple to employ these babysitters?
6. What are some of the things that they eat?
7. Why isn't the woman willing to fire the babysitters?

DISCUSSION
1. Find out how much babysitters are paid. Is this enough money for the responsibilities that they have? Should they be permitted to eat anything they want to?
2. This woman is afraid to fire the babysitters because the girls are relatives. Do you think it's a good idea to employ relatives?

LANGUAGE IN LIFE

May is often used to express permission. For example:

"You may watch television but you may not use the telephone."
(I will permit you to watch television but I will not permit you to use the telephone.)

"You may eat the apples but please don't eat the peaches."
(I will permit you to eat the apples but I would appreciate it if you would not eat the peaches.)

Agreement is expressed by saying *Yes, Of course, O.K., All right, Sure, I understand, Certainly,* or some such affirmative reply.

★ The woman writes "I have told both sitters what to eat and what not to eat." Practice expressing permission by substituting in the columns:

You may eat some	cookies
	Jell-O
	doughnuts
	potato chips
	peanut butter
	cheese and crackers
	cake
but please don't eat any	ice cream.
	tuna salad.
	luncheon meat.
	pie.
	watermelon.
	yogurt.
	caviar.

Practice in pairs. Student A expresses permission, as above, and Student B expresses agreement.

94

★★ With a partner, role-play the following conversation between a parent and the babysitter.

Parent	*Babysitter*
1. Express permission to watch television but not to use the telephone.	1. Express agreement.
2. Also express permission to listen to the radio but not the phonograph.	2. Express agreement.
3. There is some ice cream in the refrigerator. Express permission to eat some of that but not the cake.	3. Express agreement.

The parents return around midnight. The babysitter is talking on the telephone while the phonograph is playing. A half-eaten cake is on the table.

4. Express displeasure.	4. Politely explain that you misunderstood. You thought you could use the telephone but not the television, listen to the phonograph but not the radio, and eat the cake but not the ice cream.
5. Reply appropriately.	

WRITING

Now write a reply, as if you were Ann Landers, and express your opinion about this situation.

VOCABULARY

circumstances
to take advantage of
    someone or
    something
a principle
off limits
forbidden
goodies
"mine and thine"
to violate
to condone
a lack
integrity
manners
to terminate
P.S.
to hire

from the desk of ANN LANDERS

Dear Tightwad,

I telephoned Mrs. Jay Rockefeller, the wife of the governor of West Virginia, and asked what *she* would do under the circumstances. Her reply was as follows:

"No woman should allow herself to be taken advantage of—whether she's a Rockefeller or not. There's a principle involved that has to do with "mine and thine." To permit the sitters to violate that principle would be to condone a lack of integrity, to say nothing of bad manners.

"I would give the girls one more chance, ask what *they* consider a tasty snack, write it down and add a line saying that anything else is off limits. If, after that, they help themselves to forbidden goodies, I would terminate their services.

"P.S. I think the first mistake was made in hiring relatives!"

DISCUSSION

1. "What's mine is mine and what's yours is yours" is often quoted as The Code of College Roommates. You may occasionally hear a roommate misquote it: "What's mine is mine and what's yours is mine." Do you agree with Mrs. Rockefeller's principle of "mine and thine"?
2. Does her advice seem sensible, and fair to both the parents and the babysitters?

23

Housework IS Work

Dear Ann Landers,
We have three children, eight, seven, and five years of age. I am busy cleaning, cooking, baking, marketing, doing the laundry, mending, canning, taking care of the yard, and keeping two cars washed and waxed. I drive the kids to Sunday school, piano lessons, dental appointments, etc.

I am not complaining, Ann. I actually enjoy my life, but my husband is making me miserable with his insistence that I go out and get a job. He keeps yelling, "Everybody's wife is working but you!"

Do I have to get pregnant again so he'll let me stay home? Please tell me if I am "not up on the latest," as my husband insists. I feel awfully inadequate.

Lima, Ohio Problem

VOCABULARY
marketing
the laundry
mending
canning
waxed
dental appointments
to complain
miserable
insistence
pregnant
to be up on the latest
inadequate

FACTUAL QUESTIONS
1. How many children does this woman have? How old are they?
2. Name some of the things she has to do as a housewife.
3. Does she like doing these things?
4. What does her husband want her to do? Why? Do they need the extra money?
5. Is she pregnant again?
6. Why does she feel "awfully inadequate"?

CULTURAL NOTE
Is the husband exaggerating when he says that "everybody's wife is working"? Find out how many women in the United States held some kind of job outside the home in 1980.

LANGUAGE USE

"Everybody's wife is working but you" is a *generalization*. This is a common technique of argument. To generalize means to form an opinion on the basis of only a few facts. The husband has not actually counted the number of wives working. He simply generalizes from a small number of cases that he knows about.

Here are some common generalizations you may hear. How true do you think each one really is?

Women are the world's worst drivers.
There's no fool like an old fool.
The French are great lovers.
There are more beautiful girls in Texas than in any other state.
You can't teach an old dog new tricks.

DISCUSSION

1. Do you think it is a good idea for a mother of three children—5, 7, and 8—to work outside of the home?
2. Child-care centers are increasingly common in the United States. These are places in the local community where pre-school children can be taken care of while the mother is working. Are child-care centers necessary, or available, in your country?
3. In your country are wives expected or allowed to work? Does a husband feel embarrassed or ashamed if his wife has a paying job outside the home? Does a wife feel embarrassed or ashamed if she as well as her husband works?

WRITING

Write a letter, as if you were Ann Landers, in which you state your opinion about the problem from Lima, Ohio.

from the desk of **ANN LANDERS**

Dear Lima,

Apparently it's your husband who is "not up on the latest." Tell him that Lincoln freed the slaves in 1861.

The way I figure it, your husband would have had to shell out $50,000 a year if he had to pay for the services you are performing. Tell Mr. Money-Hungry that Ann Landers says he's in a semi-conscious state, and I hope he'll put a rubber band around his head and snap out of it.

VOCABULARY

to shell out
semi-conscious
a rubber band
snap out of it

CULTURAL NOTE

Ann Landers is mistaken about the date when Lincoln freed the slaves. Lincoln issued the Emancipation Proclamation in the middle of the Civil War on January 1, 1863. Slavery was not completely ended until the Thirteenth Amendment to the Constitution was adopted in 1865. Does this mistake affect your opinion of Ann Landers?

DISCUSSION

1. Is it fair to equate a wife and mother with a slave?
2. How do you suppose Ann Landers arrived at the figure of $50,000 a year? What do you think Mr. Money-Hungry's response to this figure will be?

24

What's in a Name?

Dear Ann Landers,
This friend, with whom I work on committees, insists on calling me "Mrs. Whatcha-ma-doodle." My parents came from Europe and kept the family name instead of changing it. The name is not difficult to pronounce if a person will take the time to divide it into syllables. My friends and the other people I work with have no trouble.

The last time this woman called me "Mrs. Whatcha-ma-doodle" was when she introduced me to her mother-in-law. The woman looked startled and believed it was my real name. I immediately corrected her, but with a laugh in my voice and a smile on my face. Later I mentioned the incident to a friend who said I was too sensitive, that my name *is* virtually unpronounceable, and she suggested that I grow a thicker skin. If you think she is right, say so. If not, tell me how to handle it.

Not Mrs. Whatcha-ma-doodle

FACTUAL QUESTIONS
1. Why does this woman's friend call her "Mrs. Whatcha-ma-doodle"? What does "whatcha-ma-doodle" mean?
2. Do all her friends call her by this name?
3. Why was her friend's mother-in-law startled?
4. How did the writer correct her friend?
5. What did another friend tell her about this incident?

CULTURAL NOTE
A glance through any telephone book for any city in the United States will show the variety of last names and the range of languages and countries they represent. Yet many immigrants *have* changed their names. What reasons can you think of to keep or change one's name?

VOCABULARY
to insist
startled
an incident
sensitive
virtually
a thicker skin
to handle something

LANGUAGE USE

1. A *thick-skinned* person is one who is not easily hurt by criticism or insults. A person who is sensitive and easily offended is *thin-skinned*. What do you think is the basis for this usage?

2. English has a number of colloquial expressions to be used when you cannot remember the name of someone or something. Various dictionaries record some, if not all, of the following:

For things: a *whosis* (also spelled *whoosis*)
                a *what-d'ya-call-it* (often contracted further to *whatcha-ma-call-it*)
                a *thingamy, thingamabob,* or *thingamajig*

For persons: *what's-his-name, what's-her-name*
                what-d'ya-call-him, what-d'ya-call-her (often further contracted to *whatcha-ma-call-im, whatcha-ma-call-her*)

LANGUAGE IN LIFE

★ To help people pronounce an unfamiliar name or word, it sometimes helps to do one of the following. For example, for the French name *Levesque:*

Do this	*Example*
Pronounce the name slowly, syllable by syllable	le-veck
Focus attention on the syllable that has heaviest stress	le-VECK (stress the second syllable)
Respell the name, orally or in writing	It's pronounced like L-E-V-E-C-K.
Use a familiar word that rhymes with the name	Levesque—it sounds like "a wreck."

Try to pronounce these terms in chemistry:

Spelling	*Pronunciation*	*Say*
isopropyl	/ī-so·prō-pil/	ice-a-PRO-pil
phenolphthalein	/fē-nōl·thal-ēn/	fee-nole-THAL-een
chlortetracycline	/klôr-tet·rn·sī-klin/	clore-tetra-SY-klin
trimethylpentane	/trī-meth·il·pen-tān/	try-methal-PEN-tayn
hexylresorcinol	/hek-snl·rn·zôr-sn·nōl/	hex-sul-ra-ZOR-sa-nole

Use a dictionary to learn how to pronounce the following names. Compare your pronunciation with your classmates.

Aeschylus
Simón Bolívar
Miquel de Cervantes
Chiang Kai-shek
Edgar Degas
Kahlil Gibran
Dag Hammarskjöld

Harun al-Rashid
Ando Hiroshige
Igance Jan Paderewski
Sergei Prokofiev
Sir Rabindranath Tagore
Tutankhamen
Zoroaster

Divide into pairs. Student A should look up in a dictionary the pronunciation of the place names in List 1. Student B should try to pronounce each one correctly, without looking them up. If B makes a mistake, A should correct him or her politely, give the correct pronunciation, and ask B to repeat it. Compliment or correct the pronunciation. The pair can then switch and use List 2.

List 1
Appalachia
Arkansas
Chicago
Connecticut
Memphremagog
Okefenokee
Ypsilanti

List 2
Albuquerque
Illinois
Mackinac Island
Michigan
Mojave Desert
Passamaquoddy Bay
Tucson

★★ Assume you have a friend whose name is difficult to pronounce. Use one of the following names, or use a real name in your class.

Baryshnikov   (bar-ISH-ni-kof)
Bogdanovitch   (bog-DON-a-vich)
Gauthier   (GO-te-yay)
Innamorati   (in-a-mor-AH-ty)
MacIntyre   (MAK-in-tire)
Muszynski   (ma-ZIN-ski)
Ouellette   (wa-LET)
Pizzigalli   (pit-sa-GAL-ly)
MacNamara   (MAK-nah-ma-rah)

With a partner, practice the following conversation in which A wants to introduce B to C.

A: (*Speaking to B*) I'd like you to meet C, but I'm sorry. I can't pronounce your name yet. Would you pronounce it for me again?

B: Of course. Listen. (*Pronounces name*)

A: Thank you. (*Repeats name*) I must learn that! C, may I introduce my friend, (*Says B's name again*).

Have you heard any of these expressions used? In what situations might they be *in*appropriate?

DISCUSSION

1. Do you agree with the writer—that, with a little effort, any name can be pronounced more or less correctly?
2. Have you ever had your name mispronounced by a foreigner? What was your reaction? Did you draw attention to it and try to correct it? What was his or her reaction?
3. Have you ever mispronounced someone's name and then been corrected? How did you feel? Did you make an honest effort to remember the name and to pronounce it correctly?
4. What strategy do you use to hold in your memory a name that you find difficult to remember, to spell or to pronounce?

WRITING

Write a letter to Not Mrs. Whatcha-ma-doodle, as if you were Ann Landers, and advise her how to handle this situation.

from the desk of **ANN LANDERS**

Dear Not Mrs.,

   No name is unpronounceable for those
who make an honest effort to pronounce it.
That clod who insists on calling you Mrs.
Whatcha-ma-doodle is letting you know
that you aren't worth the trouble. The
next time she does it, keep the smile *off*
your face and the laughter *out* of your
voice. Tell her if she refuses to learn how
to pronounce your name, you will be happy
to pronounce it for her—any time.

DISCUSSION

1. Do you agree that the "clod" is letting the woman know that she isn't worth the trouble? What other reasons might there be for her inability to pronounce the name?
2. Do you think Ann Landers' suggestion will work? Why or why not? What should Not Mrs. do if it doesn't?

25

Shoplifting is Stealing!

Dear Ann Landers,

Our 11-year-old son walked out of a drugstore without paying for a 39-cent pen. I suppose you would call it shoplifting, but when the item is so cheap there ought to be another word. The manager followed Charles out of the store, took him to his office, lectured him, and told him not to come into the place again. I received a telephone call asking me to come and get the child.

I have never been so burned up in all my life. That poor youngster was scared half out of his wits. When I came to get him, he was sobbing and shaking like a leaf. You'd have thought that he had stabbed the cashier and held the manager at gun point.

I think it is just dreadful that an 11-year-old boy should be made to feel like a criminal over a measly 39-cent pen.

Please tell me what can be done about sadistic store managers who would treat a small child like that. This incident might cause permanent psychic damage to my son.

A Boy's Mother

VOCABULARY
to shoplift
to be burned up
to be scared half out of
  his wits
to steal
to sob
to stab
dreadful
measly
sadistic
to treat
an incident
permanent
psychic damage

FACTUAL QUESTIONS
1. What did the mother's 11-year-old son do?
2. Was the pen expensive?
3. What did the store manager do?
4. How did the boy react?
5. Why was the boy so upset?
6. Did the boy stab the cashier?
7. What does the mother think about the store manager?
8. What does she think might happen to her son?
9. What question does she ask Ann Landers?

DISCUSSION

1. In your country, if a shopkeeper catches a person stealing something from the shop, what does he or she do? What happens to the person who is caught stealing?
2. Do you feel that the manager handled this situation wisely and fairly?
3. What would the manager have done if the boy had stolen something more valuable than a 39-cent pen?
4. Does the value of an article make any difference in the seriousness of the offense?
5. Do you agree with the mother that this incident could cause permanent psychological damage to her son?
6. Knowing Ann Landers as well as you do, what do you think she is going to tell the mother?

LANGUAGE IN LIFE

★ If this young boy had apologized to the store manager, he might have expressed his apology in any one of the following ways:

	I regret I'm sorry	that I took the pen.	
	I apologize	for	taking the pen.
(Please)	Forgive me Excuse me Pardon me		
	I regret		

Assume you have done each of the following actions. Practice making a polite apology.

1. You wake someone up by telephoning after midnight.
2. You repay a $10.00 loan a month after you promised to return the money.
3. You arrive at a meeting thirty minutes late.
4. You accidentally sit on someone's sun glasses.
5. You break a friend's expensive cigarette lighter.
6. You borrow someone's comb and lose it.
7. A classmate who was absent asks you for the homework assignment. You mistakenly tell him or her the wrong page numbers.
8. You take someone's umbrella by mistake.
9. You spill ink on a classmate's sweater.
10. Your friend demands an apology when he or she finds out that you have been spreading gossip.

★★ With a partner, prepare to role-play the following conversation between the store manager and the young boy.

	Manager		*Boy*
1.	State that you caught the boy stealing a pen. Ask if he denies it.	1.	Remain silent.
2.	Express anger. Demand an answer.	2.	Quietly admit your guilt.
3.	Ask if he knows what could happen to him.	3.	Remain silent.
4.	Demand an answer to your question.	4.	Quietly answer No.
5.	Tell him that he might be sent to jail/grow up to be a criminal/be fined $500.	5.	Apologize.
6.	Tell him that he can never come into the store again.	6.	Promise never to come into the store again.

WRITING

Write a letter to the boy's mother, as if you were Ann Landers, and reply to her request in the last paragraph.

from the desk of ANN LANDERS

VOCABULARY
merchandise
appalling
to take someone's side
grief
a mess
professional help

Dear Mother,
   Your boy was caught shoplifting and I can think of no better word to describe stealing merchandise from a store.
   I find it appalling that you attack the manager and defend the boy. A mother who takes her child's side when he breaks the law does him no favor. If this is your idea of "mother love," you're going to have a lifetime of grief and the boy will be a mess. You both need professional help—starting yesterday.

DISCUSSION
1. Do you think Ann Landers' answer will help the boy or his mother? Explain.
2. Should a parent always take his child's side (support him)?
3. What does Ann Landers mean by "professional help"? What kind is available for each? What could it do?

26

Kite Crashes Cocktail Party

Dear Ann Landers,
Last night we were invited to a cocktail party. We were hardly through our first drink when the doorbell rang and a scruffy little boy told the hostess that his kite was on her roof. Without any consideration for her six guests (some with their glasses half empty), this nut told her husband to get the ladder while she changed to sneakers. He's afraid of heights so he held the ladder while she crawled up on the roof in a cocktail dress and tennis shoes to get the kite.

The whole affair took a good half hour. I thought it was terribly rude, since we had never been in her home before and hardly knew the other guests. She could have told the brat "too bad" or "come back tomorrow."
My husband thought the whole thing was funny and advised me to forget it. I feel this woman insulted her guests and I decided to ask your opinion. What do you think?

Mad in Minneapolis

VOCABULARY

to crash (a party)
scruffy
a kite
this nut
sneakers
a ladder
to crawl
a good half hour
rude
a brat
to insult

FACTUAL QUESTIONS

1. Where did this incident take place?
2. Who rang the doorbell? Why?
3. What did the hostess do?
4. What did her husband do?
5. Why didn't he climb the ladder instead of his wife?
6. What was the hostess wearing?
7. Why does the writer think that the hostess was rude?
8. What was the opinion of the writer's husband?

DISCUSSION

1. Is it polite to leave your invited guests for any reason, especially simply to let a little boy get his kite?
2. Why do you think the writer's husband thought the whole thing was funny? Do you? Point out specific examples of humor.
3. What words or phrases in the letter reveal the writer's attitude?
4. What does the woman want Ann Landers to tell her?

LANGUAGE IN LIFE

★ When his kite came down on the roof, the little boy might have asked the hostess: "Please, ma'am. My kite just landed on your roof. Could you please help me get it down?"

There are several levels of politeness for requesting assistance. Generally speaking, a short request is less polite than a long request. *Please* can be placed at the beginning or at the end, or sometimes inserted before the verb. For example:

↑	Help me.
LEAST	Please help me.
POLITE	Will you please help me?
│	Could you please help me?
MOST	Would you be able to help me, please?
POLITE	I wonder if you could help me, please.
↓	Would you be kind enough to help me, please?

For each of the following situations, request assistance.
1. You have a flat tire. Ask a stranger to help you change the tire.
2. You need $100 quickly. Ask a friend.
3. You are lost in the city and are not sure where the bus stop is. Ask a policeman.
4. You have to carry a heavy trunk to your car. Ask a neighbor.
5. You run out of sugar in the middle of preparing a cake. Ask your neighbor for help.
6. Your frisbee lands on the roof of an unfriendly neighbor. Ask for a ladder to get it down.
7. Your car is stuck in the snow. Ask a passerby for help.
8. You are trying to force an angry, growling dog into the back seat of your car. Ask a friend to help you.

★★ Assume that the letter writer and her husband are discussing this incident after they return home. Prepare to role-play the following conversation.

Wife	*Husband*
1. Express annoyance. State your belief that the hostess was rude to leave her guests.	1. Express disagreement. State that you don't think it was rude.
2. Contradict your husband. Explain why you feel the behavior of the hostess was more than rude—it was insulting—to her guests.	2. Urge your wife to see the humor of the whole thing.
3. Express surprise. Deny anything funny about it.	3. Explain why you think it was funny: to see the hostess in a cocktail dress and tennis shoes climbing around on the roof while her husband holds the ladder. Laugh.
4. Say you do not see the humor at all—especially when she preferred to be a kite-saver for the scruffy brat rather than a polite hostess to her guests.	4. Express belief that your wife has taken the whole thing too seriously. Repeat that you think it was funny. Urge your wife to forget it.
5. State your decision to write Ann Landers and ask her opinion.	5. Encourage her to do so. Express certainty that Ann Landers will agree with you.

WRITING

Write a letter to Mad in Minneapolis, as if you were Ann Landers, and express your opinion about this matter.

VOCABULARY
to get high
otherwise
to complain

from the desk of **ANN LANDERS**

Dear Mad,
I think it's beautiful that the hostess would attach that much importance to a little boy's kite. So what if you got high a half hour later than you might have otherwise. I see nothing to complain about.

DISCUSSION

1. Do you agree that the hostess attached a great deal of importance to the little boy's kite? Might there be other reasons she climbed up on the roof to get it?
2. What was the woman so upset about? Did Ann Landers really answer the woman's question? What do you think the woman would have done if that had happened at her party?

27

Double Dinner Trouble

Dear Ann Landers,

Yesterday afternoon a pack of my husband's in-town relatives arrived (two carloads, to be exact). I was lying down, trying to take a nap after having been in the kitchen for several hours preparing dinner for 18 people who were invited the next evening.

Would you believe that my husband offered the pack of locusts the food I had prepared for my dinner party the following night? The group made hogs of themselves and wiped me out. After they left I had to clean up the mess and start cooking and baking all over again. I was in the kitchen till midnight.

My husband isn't speaking to me. He says I humiliated him because I wasn't charming and hospitable. I'd like your comments.

Mad in Wyoming

VOCABULARY

a pack
a nap
a locust
a hog
to be wiped out
to humiliate
hospitable

FACTUAL QUESTIONS

1. Whose relatives arrived?
2. How many relatives arrived?
3. Why was the woman trying to take a nap?
4. How many people were invited for dinner?
5. What did her husband do that so upset her?
6. What did the unexpected guests do?
7. What did she have to do until midnight?
8. Why is her husband angry?

DISCUSSION

1. Do you think the wife's attitude was unhospitable?
2. Do you suppose the wife will describe her 18 guests invited for dinner the next evening as "a pack of locusts" or "hogs"?
3. What social obligations does one have toward unexpected, uninvited visitors? Does the fact that they were relatives make any difference?
4. Was the husband right to offer his relatives the food?
5. What would you have done if you were the wife? The husband?

LANGUAGE IN LIFE

★ A *simile* is an expression that compares two things, using either *like* or *as*. This woman, for example, was so angry that she compares her uninvited guests to hogs or locusts. She might have said, "They were *as hungry as locusts*" or "He *ate like a hog*." There are many common similes that are regularly used in English. Try to complete each of the following comparisons. (Native-speakers of English would almost always agree, but that does not make the answer "correct." In fact, a simile that is so often used soon loses it orginality; it becomes a substitute for thoughtful, effective use of language.) Learn what is most common in English, then compare how other languages would express a similar comparison.

as + ADJECTIVE + *as* + NOUN

1. as blind as a _____
2. as busy as a _____
3. as hard as a _____
4. as white as _____
5. as cool as a _____
6. as stubborn as a _____
7. as easy as _____
8. as good as _____
9. as red as a _____
10. as flat as a _____

VERB + *like* + NOUN

1. He drinks like a _____
2. She works like a _____
3. It runs like a _____
4. She sings like a _____
5. He cries like a _____
6. She drives like a _____
7. He swears like a _____
8. It fits like a _____
9. She dances like a _____
10. He smokes like a _____

★★ With a partner, prepare to role-play the following conversation between the woman and her husband after his relatives leave.

Husband	*Wife*
1. Express annoyance. Ask how your wife could humiliate you in front of your relatives.	1. Express surprise. Ask how you humiliated him.
2. Explain how unhospitable she was, unwilling to serve all the food that was already prepared.	2. Express anger. Explain that the food was intended for tomorrow's dinner party, not for his uninvited pack of locust-like relatives!
3. Express anger. Argue that she should have been happy to see them, since they were relatives.	3. Exclaim that you were happy to see them, but not happy to see them eat everything you had spent so much time preparing.
4. Tell her that she can cook more for tomorrow, that there is still time.	4. Insist that is not the point. Argue that he had no right to offer the food that you had prepared for the dinner party.
5. Exclaim that your wife becomes silly and unreasonable after a long day, that there is no point continuing to argue with her, and that you are going to bed.	5. Reply sarcastically; he is the unreasonable one. Complain that *he* can go to bed but you have to stay up now and start cooking and baking all over again.
6. Angrily say good night.	6. Reply appropriately.

WRITING
Write a letter to Mad in Wyoming, as if you were Ann Landers, and comment on this situation.

VOCABULARY
to drop in
a victim
an obligation
to lay on a feed

from the desk of ANN LANDERS

Dear Mad,
   Husbands should keep their noses out of the kitchen unless they are doing the cooking and baking. That man of yours had no right to offer the food you had prepared for the following day. When people drop in unexpectedly, the surprised victims (host and hostess) have no obligation to lay on a feed or anything else.

DISCUSSION
1. Do you agree with Ann Landers that the husband had no right to offer the food to unexpected visitors?
2. The social rules of hospitality are different in different countries. What would have been the correct thing to do according to hospitality in your country?

28

Dream Becomes Nightmare

Dear Ann Landers,
We are a middle-aged couple who moved recently from a $20,000 cottage to a $55,000 home in suburbia. This was to be our dream house, but it is developing into a nightmare.

Minibikes are all over the place, on our lawn and in the driveway. Fireworks go off all year round, including some in our mailbox. Fathers and sons shoot birds and squirrels with BB guns. Dogs run loose in packs of six and seven, even though there is a leash law.

Minors are out at night until 11:00, yelling and screaming, making sleep impossible for those who wish to retire early. Halloween was a horror.

We don't want to move again. What can be done about this without causing bitter feelings? We'd have to talk to the parents and this would mean trouble. Or we'd have to call the police, which would be even worse. Any suggestions?

Constant Reader

FACTUAL QUESTIONS
1. Where did this couple recently move? What did they hope their new house would be?
2. What are some of the problems that they face in their new neighborhood?
3. What are their two choices, and what would be the result of each?
4. What advice do they want from Ann Landers?

VOCABULARY
suburbia
a nightmare
a minibike
a BB gun
bitter feelings
a leash law
a minor
to yell and scream
Halloween
a horror
constant

LANGUAGE USE
Many English speakers made a distinction between *a house* (any building in which people live) and *a home* (your house where you belong and feel comfortable). What do you think *a dream house* is? Why does the writer make a distinction between *a cottage* and *a home*? What would be the next higher distinction?

DISCUSSION

1. Do you think that this middle-aged couple have any children?
2. Does the writer's description of the neighborhood seem exaggerated?
3. Which of their complaints seem serious to you and should be stopped, and which could you live with?
4. Do you think it would be better to talk to the parents or the police? Why?

WRITING

Write a letter to Constant Reader, as if you were Ann Landers, and offer suggestions.

from the desk of **ANN LANDERS**

VOCABULARY

to identify
an offender
low-keyed
to appeal
decent
a right
to proceed

Dear C.R.,

Before you talk to anybody you must identify the offenders. When you are certain, talk to *them*. Don't go over with your hair on fire and yell your head off. Keep it low-keyed and appeal to them as good neighbors and decent citizens. If you get nowhere, then go talk to a lawyer. Learn what your rights are and proceed from there.

DISCUSSION

1. What kind of rights do you think a lawyer will tell them they have? What rights would you have in your country?
2. Do you think the couple will be able to talk to the offenders in a low-keyed manner? How do you think they will respond?

LANGUAGE IN LIFE

★ If this couple uses a low-keyed approach, they might appeal to the offenders "as good neighbors and decent citizens." For example, they might express a desire to find a solution that is fair to all. For example:

> I'm sure we all want to live in a community that respects the rights of everyone.
> I know you agree that firecrackers can be dangerous.
> I wonder if we can work together to solve this problem of so much noise.
> I'd like to discuss with you a problem that's been bothering me for some time.

Assume that you have one of the following problems with a roommate, neighbor, or friend. Start a low-keyed discussion by first appealing to his or her sense of fair play, and express your desire for cooperation.

1. Your neighbor's little boy deliberately pulls up flowers from your garden.
2. Your roommate keeps you awake while watching the late, late show on television.
3. Your friend often visits and stays so long that you cannot do your homework.
4. Your roommate often embarrasses you by being so loud and noisy at parties.
5. Your neighbor's child abuses your cat.
6. Your roommate regularly forgets to lock the room.
7. Your friend has borrowed $10.00, three books, a sweater and a tennis racket without returning them.
8. Your neighbors have noisy parties in their backyard, often until midnight.

★★ With a partner, prepare to role-play the following conversation between neighbors.

Neighbor 1	*Neighbor 2*
1. Express certainty that your neighbor wants to live in a reasonably neat and orderly community.	1. Agree. Proudly explain how you keep your house painted, your grass cut, and your garden weeded.
2. Agree and express thanks, but express unhappiness about (*Choose one of the following*):	
a. their children's minibikes are always left on your lawn and in your driveway.	a. Express surprise. Explain that they have been told always to put them in the garage. Agree to tell them not to leave their bikes lying around.

b. their dog digs holes in your garden and runs loose with other dogs.

b. Explain that your dog is usually tied but sometimes escapes, and that you will try to keep the dog from digging in gardens.

c. their children stay up late, run around the neighborhood and make so much noise.

c. Explain that this is only on weekends, not on school nights, but you will ask them to be more quiet on weekends.

d. their child exploded a firecracker in your mailbox.

d. Express ignorance, apologize, and agree to talk to your children about such bad behavior.

3. Thank your neighbor. Express appreciation.

3. Reply appropriately.

29

No Payoff for Goof-Off

Dear Ann Landers,
Our 20-year-old dropped out of college in the middle of this year. She says she wants to travel and mature, so that when she returns to college she will be able to appreciate what is being taught.

I say "baloney"! The girl has an excellent mind but she has goofed off, stayed up all night, slept all day, missed classes, and failed in almost every subject. Her best friend refuses to room with her next year. Our daughter owes the girl money, and she has also put the touch on her grandmother, her brother, and heaven knows who else.

My husband and I are not wealthy. We work long hours. Our home is not fully paid for. We have other children to educate. So long as our daughter stayed in college we felt an obligation to support her. Now that she has fouled up in school, I don't believe we owe her travel money while she "matures."

My husband feels we should go along with her or we might lose her for good. I believe this is subtle blackmail. He reads your column daily and thinks you're a smart woman. Please sock it to him.

The Buck Stops Here

VOCABULARY
a payoff
mature
baloney
to goof off
to put the touch on
   someone
to foul up
to go along with
   someone
for good
subtle
sock it to him
the buck stops here

FACTUAL QUESTIONS
1. Why did the girl drop out of college?
2. Does the mother agree with her daughter?
3. According to her mother, what kind of student was she?
4. Who did the girl borrow money from?
5. Does the mother feel obligated to help her daughter? Why or why not?
6. What does the father want to do?
7. Why does his wife disagree?

LANGUAGE USE

1. The woman refers to "our 20-year-old daughter." What does she mean by this? Do you think they have other children? How can you tell?
2. "To pass the buck" is an idiom meaning "to shift the blame or responsibility to someone else." The expression originated in the 19th century when a buckhorn knife was placed by a poker player to designate the dealer. If he did not want to participate in the next game, he passed the buck to the next player. Harry Truman (President of the United States, 1945–53) kept a sign on his desk: THE BUCK STOPS HERE. Why did the woman choose this signature for her letter?

CULTURAL NOTE

In the United States, unlike some other countries, post-secondary education is not free. A college/university education can be expensive. At some of the best colleges, tuition alone may be as high as $9,000 a year. However, at a state university, the tuition charges for residents of the state are considerably lower than for out-of-state students. What kinds of financial aid are available to foreign students? How important do you think the cost of the school should be in deciding where to go?

DISCUSSION

1. What is the woman asking Ann Landers? What does she want her to do?
2. Is there any reason to assume that the daughter will be more mature when she returns to college? Do you think that travel contributes to a person's maturity?
3. To what extent do you believe parents are obligated to financially support their children's education?
4. Is the writer of this letter concerned about the cost of educating her children?

LANGUAGE IN LIFE

★ With another student, prepare to role-play the following conversation between the mother and her daughter.

Daughter	*Mother*
1. Request money and explain why you want to travel.	1. Refuse, giving the reasons stated in your letter.
2. Explain why you did so poorly in school.	2. Reject these statements as "excuses."

3. Protest that parents never seem to understand/believe/trust their children.

4. Express disappointment and say that you will talk to your father "because he understands."

3. Explain why you do not feel obligated to support her travel plans.

4. Make an appropriate response.

★★ With another student, prepare to role-play the following conversation between the father and mother of this girl.

Father

1. Briefly describe the talk you just had with your daughter. Agree with some of her viewpoints.

2. Express concern that your daughter may leave for good.

3. State that you think Ann Landers would agree with your point of view.

Mother

1. Disagree with your husband. (Decide for yourself how politely or impolitely you will disagree.) Explain your reasons.

2. Protest that this is what she wants you both to believe. Explain why you regard this as "subtle blackmail."

3. Agree to write Ann Landers for advice. Say you're sure she'll agree with your point of view.

WRITING

Now write a reply to The Buck Stops Here, as if you were Ann Landers.

from the desk of ANN LANDERS

Dear Buck,
  Blackmail is the name of this game and I hope you don't fall for it. If the girl had done well in school, and you wanted to reward her with six months of travel, I'd say O.K. But she goofed off and is hoping for an escape hatch so she can avoid responsibility and do her own thing at your expense. Tell her that funds are available for school but not for an open-ended vacation. Let her know that if she agrees to return to school in the fall and puts in a productive year, you might consider giving her a summer trip as a bonus.

VOCABULARY
the name of the game
to fall for something
an escape hatch
to do her own thing
a bonus

DISCUSSION
1. Do you agree with Ann Landers? Why or why not? How is your letter different from hers?
2. Do you think the mother will agree? Will she think that Ann Landers has satisfactorily "socked it" to her husband?
3. Do you think the father will be satisfied with this response? Will he still think that Ann Landers is "a smart woman"?

30

A Question of Life

Dear Ann Landers,
My Mom is in the hospital. She is very sick. We have known for a long time that she is going to die. Three different doctors told us weeks ago. The doctors have done everything they can for Mom, but she has cancer of the bones and it has spread all over.

Mom doesn't recognize anybody. Her eyes are closed most of the time, but even when her eyes are open she doesn't see. She can't eat anything. They feed her through a needle and a rubber tube in her arm. There are needles and tubes all over. Also an oxygen machine and blood transfusion equipment. It seems like she is in pain, although the nurses say she is too doped to feel anything.

My question is this, Ann Landers: Wouldn't it be better for everybody, especially Mom, if they took all the tubes and needles out, wheeled away the bottles and blood plasma and oxygen, and just let Mom slip away to God's heavenly home?

Her Son

VOCABULARY
cancer
an oxygen machine
a blood transfusion
to be doped
blood plasma
to slip away

FACTUAL QUESTIONS
1. Why is the boy's mother in the hospital?
2. Are the doctors hopeful that she will recover?
3. What question does the boy ask Ann Landers?

LANGUAGE USE
What is a *euphemism?* When the son writes, "let her slip away to God's heavenly home," what is he really saying? What are some other common euphemisms for dying? (You might want to ask English-speaking friends.)

DISCUSSION

1. About how old is the writer of this letter? What are your reasons for thinking so?
2. *Euthanasia,* or mercy killing, means allowing, or even causing, an easy and painless death for someone who suffers from an incurable illness. "To pull the plug" is a colloquial reference to turning off the medical equipment that keeps a patient alive. It is a euphemism for *to kill,* or at least *to let die.* As modern medicine makes it possible to prolong the fact, if not the quality, of life, many complicated legal, moral, and religious questions arise. What specific questions ought to be asked? What feelings or beliefs do you have about these questions and their answers?

WRITING

Write a letter, as if you were Ann Landers, in which you answer the final question that this boy asks about his mother.

VOCABULARY

a patient
a device
bodily functions
indignity
artificial
to hold off
to deny; to be denied

from the desk of ANN LANDERS

Dear Son,

Yes, I think it would be better, but this decision is one the family must make. Doctors have to hear the suggestion from a relative. Why don't you discuss it with your family and tell how you feel—and that I agree with you.

Don't let anyone tell you that so long as there is a sign of life, there is a chance of recovery and the patient must be kept alive by every device known to medical science. When the doctors say the situation is hopeless, the patient cannot take food, no longer recognizes anyone, and is not in control of his bodily functions, I believe it is an indignity to be kept alive with needles, tubes, bottled blood, and mechanical equipment. To remove the artificial devices is not ending a life; it is the refusal to hold off death by using machinery. A person who is kept alive by machines is not living; he is simply being denied the right to die.

FACTUAL QUESTIONS

1. What is Ann Landers referring to when she refers to "this decision"?
2. Does she feel that a doctor should suggest such a decision?
3. At what point does she feel a patient should be allowed to die with dignity?
4. What distinctions does she make in the last two sentences?

DISCUSSION

1. Have you personally known a medical case of the kind that Ann Landers describes?
2. Ann Landers advises the boy to "discuss it with your family and tell them how you feel." Do you agree with this advice?
3. In the last paragraph Ann Landers explains her attitude toward euthanasia. Do you agree or disagree with her?
4. Do you think Ann Landers has had personal experience with a situation of this kind?

LANGUAGE IN LIFE

★ Assume you are the son and you take Ann Landers' advice. Prepare to explain your viewpoint and tell your family how you feel. If you wish, use the ideas and some of the language in this letter.

★★ Prepare to debate this proposition. Resolved: That euthanasia is a choice that is legally, morally, and religiously defensible.